The Journey

Per Ardua Ad Astra
Through Hardship to the Stars

The true story of a remarkable life: from childhood to retirement; from survival in wartime, to love, success and tragedy in peacetime.

by
Ted Cowling

Published by
Laundry Cottage Books

Laundry Cottage
Shawbirch Road
Admaston
Wellington
Shropshire
TF5 0AD

Tel. & Fax: 01952 – 223931

MMV © Kenneth JS Ballantyne [full text & artistic composition] & Edward A Cowling [original life material]

The right of Kenneth JS Ballantyne and Edward A Cowling to be identified as the authors of this work has been asserted by them in accordance with the Copyright, Designs and Patents Act 1988.

All rights reserved. No part of this publication may be reproduced, stored in a retrieval system, or transmitted in any form or by any means, electronic, mechanical, photocopying, recording or otherwise or in any circumstances or in any Country without the prior written permission of Kenneth JS Ballantyne or the Executors to his Estate.

First published in Great Britain in 2005 by Laundry Cottage Books, Shawbirch Road, Admaston, Wellington, Shropshire.

Contents

Page

1	Growing up and Going to War	10
2	Becoming an Airman	18
3	Bomber Command and The Flying Coffin	32
4	Coastal Command	40
5	Promotion and Sorties at Oban	52
6	His Majesty's Commission	64
7	From The White House......	73
8	......To The Kremlin	88
9	Learning to Drive whilst Learning to Fly	97
10	Bomber Command and Air/Sea Rescue	117
11	Top Gun	133
12	Peace and Matrimony	147
13	Starting Over and Making Out	160
14	In Business	167
15	Ring in the Changes	171
16	Tears and More Tears	179
17	Celebrities	183

Acknowledgements

I would like to thank all the people who have helped to turn the idea of this book into a reality. My wife Joy, without whom so much of the story would be missing and who has helped me through our years together; for her encouragement, for giving the book its title and for writing the Dedication. My friend Ken Ballantyne, who has worked so hard writing the text and transforming the notes of my story into the finished work and to his wife Elaine for proof reading it. All the various people and organisations who have consented to the use of their photographs and materials: to the family of the late Air Vice Marshall David Cecil McKinley, for permission to use extracts from his memoirs, his RAF Log Book together with the manuscript of Matthew B Wills, given to David by the author of that work; to Mr Toby Neal, Reporter with the Shropshire Star for permission to use the photographs of old Shrewsbury from the newspaper's archive book *Shrewsbury - Pictures from the Past*; to John Evans for permission to use photographs from the *John Evans Collection*; to the Book Club Associates for permission to reproduce the pictures from *World Aircraft-World War II-Part 1* by Angelucci and Matricardi; to Brockhamton Press for permission to reproduce photographs from *The Royal Air Force* by Michael Armitage; to the Promotional Reprint Co. Ltd. for permission to reproduce photographs from *Halifax and Wellington* by Bowyer and Van Ishoven and to Ken Ballantyne for permission to use his photographs of the Mohne Dam. The remaining photographs come from my own collection.

EAC

Dedication

This book is dedicated to the many thousands of men and women, from home and abroad, who served in the Allied Armed Forces, the Merchant Service and on the Home Front in World War Two between 1939 and 1945 to keep our Country free. Also to all those who have fought since 1945 to make this world a safer place. So many have died but none shall be forgotten.

"When you go home,
Tell them of us, and say:
For your tomorrow
We gave our today."

Kohima Monument Epitaph, India

The Severn Hospice

Part of the proceeds from the sale of this book will be donated to the Severn Hospice.

Severn Hospice cares for patients from Shropshire and Mid Wales with life-limiting illnesses including cancer, motor neurone disease and multiple sclerosis. We strive to provide the highest standards of nursing and medical care, to sustain quality of life and dignity and to provide patients with relief from pain. To the families, friends and carers of our patients we extend the same loving support, help and counselling, as such illnesses affect whole families.

The Hospice helps its patients enjoy a better quality of life, often enabling them to do things they thought had gone forever. It is not just a place where people go to die: many patients benefit from day hospice care and others return home following a period as an inpatient.

We are mostly reliant upon, and deeply grateful for, the contributions and generosity of local people in finding the money to keep functioning effectively and moving forward each year. We are grateful to Ted for his support and thank you for helping us by buying this book.

Lucy Proctor
Fundraising Manager
Severn Hospice
May 2005

Registered charity number 512394

Preface

This is the true story not only of a man, but of a generation, for Ted Cowling is undoubtedly a man *of* his generation and we shall not see their likes again. Born in Bethesda, North Wales in 1920, he grew up between the wars in the idyllic surroundings of Shrewsbury, the county town of Shropshire, where at the age of 10, he almost drowned in the River Severn. He went on to discover a love of flying which has remained with him to this day. He volunteered for the RAF at the outbreak of World War II and was posted to Bomber Command where he was a Leading Aircraftman Wireless Operator/Air Gunner in Fairey Battles, known unaffectionately by those who had the misfortune to fly in them, as 'Flying Coffins'. A lightly armed, single engine, slow, cramped bomber, it was already obsolescent by 1939. Sent out against the battle hardened and experienced Messerschmitt 109 pilots of Goring's Luftwaffe, it is no wonder that they felt they were flying in a coffin: so many of them were. RAF losses were disastrous and the life expectancy amongst these crews was so short, they weren't even required to salute the Officer; they would not live long enough to face a Court Martial.

Against all the odds he survived and moved to Coastal Command where, now commissioned, he was part of the hand picked crew who, in 1941, flew a highly secret and dangerous mission, arranged and approved by Churchill himself on behalf of the President of the United States of America. They were to take President Roosevelt's personal envoy and Churchill's close friend, Harry Hopkins, through the Arctic Circle to meet Joseph Stalin just days after the Nazis had turned against their former allies in Operation Barbarossa, thereby opening up the Eastern Front. The failure of this mission would have meant the total collapse of the Russian forces within a few weeks and ultimately the abandonment of the plans for D-Day. World War II would have had a very different outcome and the politics of Europe today would be unrecognisable. In his book, *Roosevelt and Hopkins*, Robert E Sherwood called Hopkins' journey, "one of the most extraordinary and valuable missions of the whole war". As the last surviving member of that crew, Ted Cowling has given us an insight into that mission, of Hopkins' meeting with Stalin and of the way the RAF crew were treated in 1941 Soviet Russia.

On his return he was sent to Canada to train as a pilot. Returning to Bomber Command in 1943 he flew Wellington bombers into the heart of German occupied Europe. After two tours of Operations he should have been given a job on the ground but such was his love of flying that he talked his way back into Coastal Command on the Air/Sea Rescue Service. Badly shot up by a Messerschmitt 110 over the North Sea one evening, short of fuel and fearing further attack, he nursed his stricken Lockheed Hudson and its crew back to Norfolk where he landed safely: he was awarded the Distinguished Flying Cross "For courage and devotion to duty on active service whilst flying against the enemy".

Thirty missions later, having now done three tours of Ops by the end of 1944 and having served King and Country with honour and distinction, he was transferred to Training Command to become a 'Top Gun' instructor at RAF Castle Combe. There, one cold and wet February night, a beautiful young WAAF whom he had not yet met saved his life. They married at the end of the war and in 2005 celebrated their diamond wedding anniversary.

He left the RAF in 1946 with the rank of Squadron Leader and entered the world of the entrepreneur. He learned his agricultural skills from a library book, and became one of the biggest wholesale seed merchants in the post war West Midlands. Ted and his wife Joy had two girls and a boy, lived in Shrewsbury and then at Allscott House, close to the grain mills he owned. He eventually sold out to Rank Hovis McDougall. He didn't even consider retirement but went back to the library, read about printing and for the next 30 years ran a very successful printing business.

In 1992 Ted and Joy lost their younger daughter to

cancer but if that was not harrowing enough, in 2000 their elder daughter also died of the same disease. Despite the shattering experience that this was for them, and one most of us cannot even begin to contemplate, they remained committed and supportive to each other and on St. Valentine's night 2003 were voted to be Britain's Most Romantic Couple at a glitzy, celebrity gala held at the Millennium Hotel in London.

At 85 he is still busy every day; he has remained as Chairman of 210 [Flying Boat] Squadron Association, is a Parish Councillor and the Chairman of the Council's Finance and General Purposes Committee.

Ted Cowling belongs to a generation whose gift of peace to those who have come afterwards, is all too often taken for granted. After The Great War of 1914-18 there was a real desire for peace, but ironically it was Hitler's rearming of Germany which provided prosperity in Britain as the factory production lines began to roll once more and ended the years of depression. World War II was not only truly global but also brought war to the British civilian population in a way it had not experienced for nearly 1,000 years. Everybody lived the war, it wasn't something that other people did for you; it touched the heart of every daily life: a whole generation gave the best years of their lives to preserve the freedom of these islands. The harsh and stark reality of history is that but for the sacrifice and courage of that generation, Britain today would be a part of the Third Reich's Nazi Empire. May that sacrifice have never been in vain nor ever forgotten.

"...the Battle for France is over...the Battle of Britain is about to begin...... Let us therefore brace ourselves to our duties and so bear ourselves that if the British Empire and its Commonwealth lasts for a thousand years, men will still say 'This was their finest hour.'"
Winston Spencer Churchill. British Prime Minister, 18 June, 1940

Kenneth JS Ballantyne	Laundry Cottage
LL.B.[Hons], Solicitor	8 May 2005

The Journey

Chapter 1

Growing Up and Going to War

"I am speaking to you from the Cabinet Room of 10, Downing Street. This morning the British Ambassador in Berlin, handed the German Government a final note, stating that unless we heard from them by 11o'clock that they were prepared at once to withdraw their troops from Poland, a state of war would exist between us. I have to tell you now that no such undertaking has been received and that consequently, this Country is at war with Germany."

Neville Chamberlain, British Prime Minister. Declaration of War and Address to the Nation. Sunday 3rd September 1939.

I lay on my bunk in the draughty nissen hut at RAF Cardington and took in the spartan surroundings that were now my home. It was Sunday evening, 10th September 1939. Those fateful words of the Prime Minister, Neville Chamberlain, broadcast to the British and Commonwealth nations just after 11 o'clock GMT a week ago, still rang in my ears. God! How long would the war last? Would we win it? What would it do to me? Would I live through it?

I thought of my two elder brothers, Albert, a regular soldier with the Royal Army Service Corps already out in Palestine and Len, with the King's Own Shropshire Light Infantry. I thought of my mother working in the Nursing Home she owned in Shrewsbury, delivering yet another baby into a Country at war once more; a war in which I now had to play my part to keep us free from the tyranny which we faced. As these thoughts tumbled through my mind, I wandered back over the years of my childhood and the happiness of growing up in the Shrewsbury of the 1920s and 1930s.

I had been born in Bethesda, North Wales, on 23 February 1920, the third of four children; Albert, Len, me, and my sister Pat. Our mother was a mid-wife and our father a Dispenser and not long after my fourth birthday we had moved to Shrewsbury, to a smart house in Coton Hill. In 1938 we moved again to the other side of town, near Porthill.

Looking up Shrewsbury's Pride Hill from St John's St and Shoplatch showing the now demolished Victorian market building (left) and Threatre Royal (right)

Shrewsbury was much smaller then than it is now but in many ways it was much busier. Sentinel–Cammell, later Rolls Royce, had the Sentinel Works at Harlescott and was the jewel in the Town's manufacturing crown. Many young men from Shrewsbury and far beyond, longed to serve their apprenticeship at the Sentinel–Cammell factory which at that time made steam engines. One very reluctant apprentice in the 1930s though was Kenneth More, who happily left Sentinel and went on, after a wartime career as a Naval Officer, to become one of our best-loved and quintessentially English actors.

The livestock market was near the river where the bus station and Raven's Meadow car park now stands, which is why that road is known as Smithfield Road. The abattoir for the market stood on the corner by what is now the entrance to the Riverside Shopping Centre and CR Birch & Son the ironmongers, still stands and trades today from their shop on the corner of Roushill and Smithfield Road. Mr Birch and later his son, both played cricket for Shropshire. The animals coming to the market were brought on foot by drovers, presumably employed by the livestock market, and were driven through the streets of Shrewsbury each market day.

Only a few cars were to be seen driving up and down Pride Hill. It wasn't yet the choking, stinking, daylong traffic jam it was to become in the 1970s before the much-needed pedestrianisation. The shops in Pride Hill were all family businesses with character and charm, happily lacking the corporate anonymity of today's town centres up and down Britain.

As a child I would go into these shops with my mother, who was nearly always dressed in her Nurse's uniform. She knew all the staff in each one we visited, having delivered most of their children for them, and was greeted with a cordial, "Good morning Nurse Cowling, and how is Mr Cowling today." Inwardly I would groan as we went through the same courtesies we had just been through with Mrs Evans in the cheese shop and Mrs Pearman in the bread shop. I was impatient to get back home so that I could go out to play with my brothers and friends.

The River Severn, Shrewsbury close to where I nearly drowned

The River Severn was of course a great attraction for us as youngsters, especially near the Severn Roughs where the bed of the river allowed us, when the water was low enough, to play in the middle. We swam, we played, we splashed; we were young children attracted by the fatal charm of cool water on a hot summer's day. Aged 10, I carelessly swam out from the warm shallows and felt icy cold fingers tug eagerly at my muscles. In no time I was slipping deeper into the water, being pulled away by the silent, sly, silky current. I was going under; I tried to cry out but my voice wouldn't work; I tried to swim back but my legs wouldn't work. Slowly I felt the river wrap her cold, dark cloak around me – but I didn't care any more.

Suddenly the sun was shining again and Len had hold of me, pulling me, coughing and choking, towards the bank. He laid me on my front and frantically squeezed the water out of my lungs. He was sobbing as he worked to save my life. Afterwards he told me the sobbing was at the thought of the thrashing he would get when he got home if I died. But on that innocent summer afternoon in 1930, my older brother Len saved my life and I have never forgotten it.

A year later I showed my first stirrings for the RAF when I climbed a tree, taking an umbrella with me. When I had reached a respectable height I opened the umbrella and jumped off the branch shouting, "Look Len, I'm a parachutist". I hit the ground with a sickening thud, twisted my ankle and put a hole in my knee that needed four stitches from my father and a dressing from my mother to patch me up. Once again Len was unimpressed as he had to help me home, a trail of blood showing where we had been. Fortunately, this was to be the only time that I attempted to use a parachute.

Not long afterwards, Len and I were walking along Corporation Avenue when an eccentric old sod, best avoided if possible, rushed out of the alley by his house and hit me on the top of my head with what was left of his mop. The edge of the circular metal mop clamp had caught me and left a gash which poured blood. At home, father got his needle and catgut out again; eight stitches this time.

In 1931 at the age of 11, I just took this as all part of the rough and tumble of growing up and my parents never doubted it. Today, in the litigation culture we endure, the old chap would have been prosecuted, sentenced, sued for what he didn't have and a claim would have been made for me to the Criminal Injuries Compensation Board. All in all the tax-payer would end up picking up a hefty bill for what was really no more than part of the rich tapestry of life. Life is not without risk, it is from our mistakes and mishaps that we learn what to avoid and what to court. As the saying goes, 'Nothing is a complete failure, it can only serve as a bad example'.

These were halcyon school days in the peaceful and seemingly trouble free years of the late 1920s and early 1930s. By 1936, at age 16, I was already fascinated by aeroplanes and on 23 May that year my father took me to RAF Tern Hill for Empire Air Day to see the 'planes. I was hooked. Inevitably, idyllic though it was, my childhood came to an end and I had to earn a living. I became an articled pupil to Arthur E. Williams, an Architect and Chartered Surveyor of Dogpole, Shrewsbury and assisted with the design of many well-known public houses in Shrewsbury and the surrounding area. My design work was chiefly to do with public houses as Mr. Williams had contracts with the Wolverhampton and Dudley Brewery and Trouncer's Brewery of Shrewsbury.

Mr. Williams employed eight members of staff; two of his assistants being his son, Peter and Peter's friend Eric Webb, both educated at Shrewsbury School. It was whilst at school that Peter and Eric applied to the fledgling RAF for a short service commission and both became Pilot Officers, flying at weekends from RAF Station Wittering in Cambridgeshire. Although they were older than me, I became very friendly with these two lads and at the age of about 17 I persuaded them to take me to Wittering and go up with them in an Anson aircraft as they practiced 'circuit and bumps' (landings and take-offs). There was little or nothing on the aeroplanes of 1937 that was automatic and even the undercarriage had to be manually wound up and down. I was so thrilled at the time when they allowed me to perform this fairly arduous task on the downwind leg prior to their approach to land. I felt like I was really one of the crew.

The Avro Anson

They both survived the war and remained in the RAF afterwards. Peter made Air Vice-Marshall but sadly died in Australia from cancer some time ago. Eric made Wing Commander and died in the late 1990s.

By now it was 1939 and the storm clouds of war had once again gathered across Europe. Hitler's Nazis were in power in Germany and Mussolini, Il Duce, had ruled Italy since 31 October 1922. In 1936 we had watched the Pathe newsreel pictures in the cinemas of the carnage in the Spanish civil war which had brought General Franco to power. The same year Pathe News had also brought us a foretaste of what was to come, when it showed Hitler ostentatiously leaving the Olympic Stadium in Berlin rather than present the black American athlete Jesse Owens with any of the 4 gold medals he had won on the track. In 1937 the Japanese had captured Shanghai and the following year they occupied Canton. Also in 1938 Nazi Germany invaded Austria; Britain mobilised the Royal Navy and, thanks entirely to the wisdom and foresight of Air Chief Marshall HCT Dowding, introduced the Spitfire and Hurricane fighter planes to the RAF, putting them into production at Lord Beaverbrook's factories.

Wyle Cop, Shrewsbury

Flying had got into my blood and the looming war gave me the chance to join the RAF and become airborne: I was going to be a pilot. On Monday 4 September 1939, like a moth to a candle, I was drawn to the new Royal Air Force Recruiting Centre recently opened at the old Wyle Cop School in Shrewsbury. I was taken into a room and put in front of an elderly Flight Lieutenant, who was wearing the 3 medals from World War 1, affectionately known by the troops as 'Pip, Squeak and Wilfred'. He wrote my name, age and address on an official form and I was told to sit outside on a bench in the passage and wait to be called for my medical. Soon I was removing my jacket and shirt; the Doctor put his fingers on each side of my chest, tapped the back of his hand and said, "hmm"! I was then asked to turn around and he carried out the same procedure to my back. I then felt the ice cold disc of his stethoscope on my skin as he checked my heart. He asked me to breathe in and out deeply, to turn round and face him and do the same whilst he listened to my chest. I was then asked to sit on a chair, pull up my trousers and cross my legs. I was promptly hit just below my left kneecap with a rubber mallet and then, after I had crossed over my other leg, he repeated the exercise. A short time later about 10 or 12 of us together were lined up and asked by the doctor to drop our trousers, cough twice and that was that: we were deemed medically fit for the RAF.

The successful applicants were shown to another room and the Officer we had met on arrival handed us a Bible. In a quiet voice he asked us to repeat after him that we would uphold the principles of the Royal Air Force and serve His Majesty the King obediently etc.etc. We were each handed the form he had completed and told to sign it: I was now AC2 Cowling, number 937262, an 'erk' in His Majesty's Royal Air Force. I was given a railway warrant to RAF Cardington and cheerfully made my way home to break the news of what I had done to mum and dad. I was 19.

Chapter 2

Becoming an Airman

A few days later my father took me to Shrewsbury Railway Station and saw me off on my journey to RAF Cardington in Bedfordshire. I had said goodbye to my mother at home: she could not bear to come to the station to see another of her children go to war: her heart was breaking. I found a compartment with a couple of other chaps in it who, it turned out, were also going to RAF Cardington. As I leaned out of the window to wave goodbye to my father, he stood close to the carriage door and said quietly, "Don't forget to write to your mother, Ted." In that moment I saw the strain etched across his face; his memories of the 1914 – 1918 conflict still haunted him. Then a whistle blew from somewhere near the back of the train and the platform superintendent waved his green flag towards the drivers cab: steam hissed and poured out across the platform from the valves of the big GWR engine in a deafening crescendo. Its whistle blew and split the air as the great driving wheels began to turn and eased us forwards: we were off. Smoke and soot belched from the funnel and settled on the waving crowd; the silent tears of mothers and girlfriends leaving pink watery tracks through the film of coal dust on their cheeks. With another roar of steam the powerful engine slowly slipped past the platform, clouds of billowing smoke huffing from its funnel. As I hung out of the window, my father, still clutching his ½d platform ticket, raised his arm in farewell and then, enveloped by the steam, was gone. I wondered if I would ever see him again.

Five hours later, and in somewhat better spirits, about fifteen of us arrived at Cardington Railway Station. This was the start of our great adventure but as we stumbled out of various compartments onto the noisy platform, laughing and joking we were greeted with the bawling voice of an RAF Corporal. "Come on *Gentlemen,* fall in," he shouted. With a swing of his cane he said, "I can see we'll have to smarten you lot up. When you speak to me you will call me Sir; 'cos I say so. Now by the left, quick march." We swaggered along the platform to a waiting 15cwt truck and were ordered to climb into the back; luckily it had a canvass cover because there were no seats and we had to stand up. As we rumbled away from Cardington Station a lot less sedately than we had left Shrewsbury Station, I looked back towards the train which was now pulling out for the next part of its journey. I suddenly realised that it would be a long time before I saw home again.

We pitched and rolled about in the back of that truck for what seemed an eternity, until some time later it pulled up with a jerk. We all grabbed each other to save being thrown to the floor. A body-less head appeared over the tailboard; it was the Corporal. "Come on there, get down and report yourselves to the Guardroom." Completely worn out and carrying our cases we were met by a Sergeant wearing a cap covered in red cloth – our first encounter with the Royal Military Police. His boots were so highly polished I could see my face in his toecaps. "Where have you brought this rabble from, Corporal? Leave your cases outside and go and book yourselves in", he bellowed. I began to wonder whether anyone in the RAF spoke at normal volume.

Duly booked in we left the Guardroom again, picked up our cases and the Corporal marched us across the parade ground. Halfway across he stopped us, "At ease", he said. We had stopped in the centre of a large area of tarmac. "Well," he said, "this is where we'll meet every morning at 08.00 hours. By the time I'm finished with you lot you will be fit to take on Tommy Farr." (Tommy Farr was a famous Welsh boxer of the day). He called us to order and we marched, if one could call it marching at this stage, to a long hut. We climbed the steps and filed through the doorway and into a large room. It resembled a dormitory with twelve beds, lockers and chairs down each side of the room. In the middle there was a black upright solid fuel stove the chimney of which disappeared through a hole in the roof. This was to be our home for the next six weeks. The door we had passed on our left when we came in was 'God's Room'; it was the Corporal's private quarters and lo and behold anyone who entered without his permission, he told us. At the far end of the room there was a third door leading to yet another room – the ablutions. There were six flushing toilets with a partition between each but no fronts, six hand basins and one open shower. There was no privacy – this was the RAF.

I managed to get the bed in the far corner on the left of the room and the furthest away from 'God's Room'. We had barely put our cases down when the Corporal told us to "Stand by your beds". This phrase, which is branded into the brain of anyone who has ever been in the Services, meant immediately stand to attention at the foot of your bed, one foot away, irrespective of how you were dressed or what you were doing. The Corporal cheerfully explained that when he walked into the room he would shout *'Stand by your beds'*, because he was in charge. If any of us didn't obey him, there was always the job of washing down the hut steps with cold water every morning for seven days, before breakfast; and if more than one of us failed to obey him they too would wash the steps in turn, even though they had been washed just a minute before.

We were soon marched to the Quartermaster's stores to obtain our mug, knife, fork and spoon and then marched again to the Airmen's Mess for a well earned cup of 'char' and baked beans on toast. For some unknown reason we were allowed to wander back to our billets on our own, much to the relief of us all. Back at the billet I unpacked my case and placed my underwear, socks, razor, tooth brush and tooth paste etc in the locker and pushed my case, out of sight of the Corporal, under the bed. Many of the other erks had already made up their bed and settled down, which I thought was a good idea. The mattress consisted of three blocks of material, which felt as if they were filled with hay or straw, but I never found out. Three blankets were provided and a hard pillow; there were no sheets. This was my bed and hard though it was it was far better than sleeping on the floorboards.

Someone had already got the upright stove in the middle of the hut going and was regularly stoking it up from the pile of coke outside the far door of the ablutions. As I lay on my bed thinking about how I had got here, some of the other erks were sitting around the stove on their chairs whilst the rest, like me, were lying on their beds talking or reading. The hut was warm and friendly. It felt safe. Our hut was now occupied by 24 of us, and we became a very close-knit bunch of fellows. We were all home sick, but we became very friendly and most importantly we quickly learned to look out for one another. Although we really did not like the attitude of the Corporal, in time we all grew to appreciate him because he was making men out of the boys he had been given. This is what the Service required and what the Country needed. We were after all at war, not on holiday.

No enemy bomb could have shattered the peace and quiet as instantly and successfully as Corporal Simkiss did that evening. There was an almighty bellow, *"Standby your beds."* We were all up like a shot out of a gun, standing to attention, at the foot of our beds. The Corporal spoke; "Lights out will be at 22.00 hours. I hope you all sleep well. Reveille at 06.00 hours, breakfast 06.30 hours to 07.30 hours. Normally you will assemble outside the hut at 07.45 hours for parade at 08.00 hours, but tomorrow you will become airman when you will be issued with your uniforms and you are to be ready to move off to stores at 08.30 hours. Goodnight to you." He walked back into his quarters. Many of us were tired after our long day, so the majority lay back on top of their beds to idle the time away until 'Lights Out'. It was now 21.30 hours and I was ready for bed. I was half asleep and thinking, 'Oh what have I done', when I fell into a blissful sleep.

I was awakened by the sound of a bugle, Reveille; it was time to get up. I had slept all night. I opened my eyes to the noise of the fire in the middle of the room being fed with coke. Someone else put the lights on and I was out of my bed pulling on my Y-fronts. I picked up my razor, towel, soap, toothbrush and paste and joined the queue in the ablutions. After a brisk wash and shave, I returned to my bed and put on the clothes I had laid out on my chair the previous night. I put on my shoes and plastered brylcreem on my hair, going back to the ablutions to comb it in the mirror on the wall. I had forgotten my stand-up toilet mirror which mum had bought me the day before. About eight of us were now already dressed and on our way each with mug and cutlery, to sample our first full meal from the RAF kitchen.

The Airmen's Mess was full of young men in uniform, some eating at the long tables and others in a queue waiting to receive their food. Being in civilian clothes we were stared at and there was shouts of 'rookies'. We took our place and when it became my turn I picked up a bowl in front of a very large hot plate behind which stood an airman, with an open neck collar and wearing a chef's white hat. He dipped the ladle he was holding into a very large bowl which contained a steaming hot mixture and poured it into my dish which I had placed with both hands in front of him. I felt like Oliver Twist. With a smile, he hoped that I enjoyed the breakfast and I went and sat next to my mates. The porridge was quite pleasant actually, although less water and more milk would have improved it, but I was just thankful for small mercies. I had no complaints and anyway it felt good in my stomach. I returned my empty bowl to the table littered with other empty bowls where another airman, who was obviously on 'jankers', was collecting them for washing. I returned to the queue, picked up a plate in front of another huge hot-plate and was served with two large slices of bacon, a big spoonful of egg substitute, baked beans and some rather runny hot tomatoes. I added two slices of toast and returned to my seat. The meal, although it did not look like mum's cooking, was very nourishing and I ate the lot. I kept one piece of toast to be covered with a large dollop of margarine and a similar amount of marmalade from two plates on the table and drank a mug of pleasant tea which I had previously collected from the urn.

Walking back to our billet we were now fit for anything that Corporal Simkiss threw at us. It was 08.20 hours and the 24 occupants of Hut 1 assembled outside. The Corporal appeared, smartly dressed with a white belt around his waist and his cane in his hand, he called us to order as we placed ourselves in two lines. Corporal Simkiss then shuffled us around so that the smallest would lead and the tallest would be at the rear. Once satisfied, he told us that this was to be our position at all times on parade, then tested us out – *"At ease"*, on this command we were permitted to stand with our feet apart. *"Atten-shun"*, feet together and stand erect. He practised this on us several times and when satisfied said "Good. Let's go. *Atten-shun!"* he bawled, "by the left, quick march". We were on our way to the Quartermaster's stores again, this time to be given our uniforms and become real airmen.

After stepping out along the concrete roadways for five minutes to another part of the camp, we arrived at a large building with two sliding doors. Whilst we stood at ease, the Corporal went in for a few moments before sending us in four at a time. Inside, the room was so large it resembled a small hanger with a very long counter, behind which stood six or seven airmen and in the background I saw a Warrant Officer and a Flight Sergeant looking at us quizzically. We were first issued with kit bags and then three Sergeants and a Corporal measured us for size. Uniforms, trousers, shirts, underpants, long john's, tie, black boots, socks etc; they were all put in our kit bags. A forage cap was handed over the counter to me. "Try that for size, lad," said the Sergeant. Size 7 and too small, so he passed a slightly larger size to me, which fitted perfectly on the side of my head. Gas masks were issued next, with instructions to carry them at all times, even when going to the Mess or NAFFI. So with the kit bag and gas mask over my shoulder and the other erks kitted out, we were marched back to our hut to get changed into our new uniforms.

It was good to see us all in uniform; we were all one, a team. Of course there were a few moans at first, the trousers were very rough on the legs and the boots were so heavy and uncomfortable, but we soon got used to them. We all looked very smart and proud of ourselves and smelt very new. My civilian clothes were hidden in my case under the bed ready to take home later.

To get accustomed to our new life Corporal Simkiss released us from duty until 14.00 hours during which time most of us visited the NAFFI to enjoy a decent mug of tea and a NAFFI rock bun, which cost four old pennies [about 1½p now]. It was a valuable chance to sit there, talking and getting to know from each other what we did in civvy-street. I had met up with a grand bunch of fellows, most of who wanted to fly. Well we would soon know what our future would be as Corporal Simkiss had already told us that we would be attending an interview that afternoon.

Lunch was over and at 14.00 hours we were marched to Station Headquarters where we gathered in a large nissen hut. With my cap removed, for at that time I didn't know exactly how to salute an Officer, those of us who had volunteered for flying duties were taken to a smaller room off the nissen hut to take an education test. Additions, fractions and decimalisation questions had to be answered together with some general knowledge questions such as who was the Chancellor of the Exchequer, who was the Leader of the opposition, what was the capital of America, Australia, France and Germany? What did I do in civvy-street? Why did I want to join the RAF? And so on. A Flying Officer, who reminded me of a schoolmaster and was about 60, interviewed me and told me that I had passed the education test with flying colours. "What career do you want in the RAF, Cowling?" "I want to be a pilot, Sir," I said. He looked sad and said, "I'm sorry son, at the moment we urgently need aircraft crews." I was devastated; I had so wanted to be a pilot like my friends

Peter and Eric. He then said, "Why don't you become a Wireless Operator/Air Gunner? After taking your course you will be able to fly immediately." I thought, well at least I'll be able to fulfil some of my ambition and fly. "Yes please Sir, I'll do it," I said. He got up, shook my hand and wished me good luck. Little did I know then how much I would need that luck.

That night I did what my father had asked me to do as he had said goodbye on Shrewsbury station, I wrote home to my mother to let her know I had arrived safely. Now that I was wearing my RAF uniform I was thoroughly enjoying myself. I was sure mum and dad would be proud of me and I had also heard a rumour that we would be home for 7 days leave after our square bashing course. Only another six weeks and I could go home and show off my uniform. That would be good for the girls.

The following six weeks were the most strenuous of my life. Parade every morning followed by exercises and learning how to salute an Officer. "Right, watch me", bawled Corporal Simkiss. "*One*, swing your right arm up, so that the palm of your hand is facing the front, with your fingers nearly poking your right eye out, *pause*, and *two*, bring your arm smartly down to your side. Remember, 'long way up, short way down'. Now you do it." This is how we learnt to salute an Officer sitting down or standing before him and if passing, use the same technique but turning our heads slightly in the Officer's direction. We were also taught that it was not the man in the uniform whom we were saluting, but the uniform itself; it was the King's uniform – "and don't you ever forget it!"

Marching was continuous, for hours on end until, as a squad, we got it right. Slow marching for funerals or state occasions, standard marching for parade and even running at the double were all included. Then in the afternoons we stripped down for P.T. My bones ached; I had not done so much activity since I was at school. I was now becoming very fit - so where was Tommy Farr? We played football on Thursday afternoons and afterwards got a shower in our billets. I was now really enjoying life in the RAF; it was difficult to remember that we were a Country at war.

As we became much more efficient on the parade ground, so we were trusted with a weapon and were issued with Lee Enfield rifles from the armoury. This brought a whole new dimension to marching. It was so different with a rifle in your hands to stand to attention, slope arms, change arms, present arms, stand at ease and so on. It soon all became automatic to us and although I say it myself, I consider we became a very efficient and smart squad indeed.

We were nearing the end of our stay at Cardington when the news reached us that in the early hours of 14 October 1939 the German U-boat U-47, skippered by Lt. Commander Gunther Prien, had crept past the supposedly impenetrable defences at Scapa Flow in Orkney and had torpedoed the World War I veteran battleship HMS *Royal Oak*. The Country was stunned by this audacious attack and it was a reminder to us all why we were here. Prien and his crew made it safely back out to sea and returned to Germany to a heroes' welcome. They were flown to Berlin where Hitler awarded Commander Prien the coveted Knight's Cross.

Today, the *Royal Oak* still lies on the sea bed at Scapa Flow and is off limits to divers: the wreck is a war grave as the bodies of most of the 833 sailors and civilian workers who died on her that night, are still in her. Neither Gunther Prien nor U-47 survived the war. They were sunk on the night of 7/8 March 1941 whilst attacking convoy OB293.

The day before we left we received instructions to report to the Orderly Room. Standing outside the door I heard, 'Cowling 262' being called (this number was the last three digits of my service number). I entered the room and was handed a railway warrant. This would take me home to Shrewsbury and eight days later would allow me to take a train from Shrewsbury to my new posting.

The following day we all said our farewells to Corporal Simkiss and thanked him for his patience with us and for making men out of those boys he had been given. He had done a good job on us and we had not let him down. I even detected a small tear in his eye because despite his rough exterior, he was a decent chap. In retrospect though I think it was simply a case that he knew many of us would not live to see the end of the war. Fortunately at that time we were all innocently oblivious to what lay ahead. Once more we jumped into the back of the 15cwt outside the Guardroom and we were on our way to the railway station and home.

It was mid-October 1939 and Britain was in the midst of the phoney war. I hadn't told my parents exactly when I would be home because the railways were unbelievably busy and a little chaotic. These were the days before railway nationalisation and all the five big train companies, The Great Western Railway [GWR], The London, Midland, Scottish Railway [LMS], The London and North Eastern Railway [LNER], The Southern Railway [SR] and The Caledonian Railway [CR] all ran to their own time-tables without linking up with the others – just like today really.

Troops were being moved all over the Country and the stations were bristling with uniforms, much more so than 6 weeks earlier when I had left to join the RAF. Soldiers, sailors and airmen; some were coming home on leave and being greeted with smiles and laughter, others were leaving and being seen off with tears and silent prayers. Children were being evacuated from the towns and cities to the relative safety of the countryside and all around me they sat or stood, their brown labels tied to their coats. Some had tear stains on their cheeks, some simply had mucky faces either from life in the city or soot from the steam engines - it was difficult to tell which, but they all had the same blank expression, not really understanding why they were being taken away from home.

The debacle of Norway, the defeat and miracle of

Dunkirk, the victory of the Battle of Britain, and the Blitz, all lay ahead in 1940, but towards the end of 1939 it was difficult to reconcile the relative calm we were experiencing, with a nation at war against an army which had just set Europe on fire. The weather was lovely and warm for the time of year and people strolled in the pleasant autumn sunshine, unaware of the harshness of the winter to come or the hardship of the war ahead. The expected air raids and gas attacks hadn't materialised and there was a surreal feeling to the activity going on.

Evacuees waiting for a train to the country

Those eight days of leave were wonderful and I felt that I had really earned them. I arrived in Shrewsbury in the late afternoon. The station, like all the stations, was bustling but Shrewsbury was always particularly busy during the war because it was the main line junction from Wales and fed into the railway hub of Crewe and the Manchester conurbation. As the train slowed and I felt the brakes begin to bite on the iron wheels, I jumped up from my seat, pulled my kit bag and the suitcase I had brought from home which now held my civvy clothes, off the luggage rack and slid open the heavy compartment door. There was a group of KSLI soldiers at one end of the coach standing by the door. "Which side is the platform?" I asked. A fresh-faced lad even younger than me looked round and answered, "This side, mate. You getting off here too?" "Too right I am", I replied and turned back to the compartment. "Come on Jack," I said, "we're here", and with that I grabbed my kit bag and case and moved to where the KSLI lads had already got the carriage door open wide.

The noise of the station and the white steam from the engine wafted into the carriage through the open door. That lovely evocative smell of burning coal and boiling water that only comes from steam engines, filled the corridor. People were already running along the platform keeping pace with the slowing train, waving and calling to the young men and women in uniform they had come to meet. Whistles blew on other platforms for other trains and porters shouted, "Stand clear, please. Mind the doors".

As the train pulled alongside the platform, one by one we jumped from the doorway into this cauldron of bodies and noise. I swung my kit bag over my shoulder and walked towards the steps and the way out, through the thin veil of steam that was rising from under each of the carriages. As I emerged from the gloom into the autumn sunshine and walked up Castle Foregate, I felt 10 feet tall. Last time I was here I was a civilian, now I was in my sky blue RAF uniform. Jack and I walked up the hill keeping pace with a brown and white Shire horse which was straining between the shafts of a cart making the last deliveries of the day before the chill of the evening air rose from the river. A couple of girls whistled at us and we smiled at them in return; this was going to be good.

I thought that my mother would never stop crying. I was the first in the family to join the RAF and she said how smart I looked – but I think she was just relieved to have her youngest son back home again, even if only for a few days. I had arranged to meet Jack that night in town. We had a couple of beers and then decided to go and see Shirley Temple in *Little Miss Broadway*. We met up with two pretty girls in the queue and joined them for the film. The next day was Saturday so we fixed a date to meet them at 2o'clock and take a boat ride on the river. Later that evening we sat with the girls in the lounge bar of The Plough in The Square (sadly no longer a pub); out of the wireless set on the wall, the mellow tones of Artie

Shaw and his Orchestra playing Begin the Beguine, filled the air. The American dance bands were becoming very popular with the young Service recruits and it gave the pub a lovely atmosphere. It was so strange to be doing all these normal, peacetime activities when we were supposed to be at war. "Enjoy it while you can Ted," said Jack as we sat drinking a beer with the girls, "There'll be plenty of time for war before this lot's over." Two years later Jack's Wellington bomber was shot down on a night raid over Hamburg and he was killed along with the rest of the crew.

Eight days after I had arrived at Shrewsbury station I was on my way again, this time to Wireless School. The course was very intensive and we had little time for fun. We sat in the classroom for most of the day and when we weren't, we were flying. The object of all this training was to teach us the fundamentals of the radio communications set, the phonetic alphabet, Morse Code, both on sound and by light, how to obtain fixes, the principle of QDM and so on. One foggy day in 1944 I would be very glad that I had listened to the QDM lectures; it would save my life and that of my brother Len. When we had qualified we were issued with what we called a 'spider'. It was the cloth emblem which we stitched to our sleeve to indicate to all the world that we were qualified wireless operators.

It was now time to go to Gunnery School at Porthcawl. We were first taught how to fire the Lewis Gun, to dismantle it and clean it. Then on to the .303 Browning machine gun; how it worked, how to dismantle it and replace all the parts, how to correct a jam or misfire. After we had got the hang of doing this with our eyes open, we then had to do it wearing a blind-fold. The reason for this was simply that at night, over enemy territory the only light available to us would be from the stars – if there were any. My own life and the lives of the rest of the crew might one day depend on my ability to perform these tasks quickly and efficiently in the pitch dark. We were taught how to fire at a moving target and for this purpose for one week I was positioned in the bowels of a

Hampden light bomber aircraft firing at a drogue being towed by a Fairey Battle.

Alton Towers' worst ride has nothing on the gun position in the Hampden. I was seated in a large glass bubble of a compartment strapped under the body of the aircraft. I could see all around and if I looked down I could even see the sea far below. I thought, "I must have been mad to volunteer for this. What the hell have I let myself in for?" Once more I finished this course with an above average score and was presented with my brass bullet to wear on my arm along with the 'spider'. I was now a fully operational Wireless Operator/Air Gunner and all ready to defend my Country against the enemy.

Being fully qualified and passing out above average, I was promoted to the rank of Leading Aircraftsman, which is equivalent to a Lance Corporal in the army. A cloth propeller was stitched to both the sleeves of my tunic and I was now earning four shillings a day with one shilling flying pay. At this time petrol was 11½d a gallon and a packet of 20 Players cigarettes the same price. If you put a shilling in the cigarette slot machine, a packet of 20 would drop down in a cellophane wrapper and inside the wrapper was your half penny change. Woodbines were 2d for five, beer 6d a pint, postage on a letter was 1d (one class only – first) and a Ford 8 saloon motorcar could be bought for £98-19-6d including purchase tax.

Chapter 3

Bomber Command and The Flying Coffin

At the end of my course at the Gunnery School in Porthcawl, I received my Operational posting. It was RAF Station Duxford near Cambridge. I reported to the Orderly Room at Porthcawl and was issued with my travel warrant to Cambridge Railway Station. After a long and tedious journey from South Wales to London and then across the city and another train to Cambridge, I duly reported to the Orderly Room at Duxford. It looked just the same as the one I had left at Porthcawl; even the impassive expression on the face of the Military Police Corporal was the same.

I was shocked into a reality check by all the flying activity taking place. Spitfires were taking off and landing at fairly regular intervals. One or two were even showing bullet holes and damage from contact with the enemy over the English Channel. The occasional Fairey Battle and Blenheim 1V light bombers were coming in too. In that moment I realised that I was now on an operational station. My stomach turned over as I thought, "I'll soon be flying in one of those 'kites'". I thought of my mother and of how worried she must be; remembering that she had been through all this once before only 20 years or so ago; wondering whether my father would ever come home: and now all three of her boys were away. I thought again of my father's words to me when I first left home back in September, "I'll ring her tonight to let her know I'm still in the land of the living," I resolved.

The Airmen's billet was situated in one of the several fine Georgian blocks on the Station. There I met a number of airmen with the same rank as myself, who, despite the so called 'phoney war' most people had enjoyed that autumn, turned out to be battle worn already. I was given a bed similar to that at Cardington but this time with sheets: I was now aircrew and there were at least a few privileges. I took off my tunic and unpacked my kitbag into my locker. As I hung my greatcoat in a type of wardrobe by my bed, I settled down with the men who were now my mates. They quickly told me about the two most important things I needed to know – life on the Station and the girls in Cambridge.

They quietly made me feel very welcome. It is difficult to convey now, how important that was for us all. On an Operational Station no one knew how long anyone would be there. In the front line of aerial combat, where bombing missions were flown nearly every day, 'here today and gone tomorrow' took on a whole new meaning. Although Barnes Wallis's fast and manoeuvrable two-engine Wellington bomber was in service in Bomber Command in 1939, the MKI having had its first flight on 23rd December 1937, the four-engine Lancaster had not yet been developed from the smaller Manchester and there just weren't enough Wellington's to go round. Consequently, most of the RAF's bombers in 1939 and early 1940 were the early 1930's generation and were generally out-powered and out gunned by the enemy. Aircrew losses were high. That is why there was such a shortage, but that bandit of a Flying Officer at RAF Cardington hadn't told me that when he said that being aircrew would let me fly very soon!

About an hour later a Flight Sergeant walked in to the billet: no one moved. 'Stand by your beds' was for recruits, not operational aircrew. He said, "Cowling 262, put your tunic on and come with me, I'll take you down to the Flights." Pulling on my tunic and with my gas mask over my shoulder I walked with him past more Georgian buildings and down to the Flight Office.

This was a smallish room carved out from the corner of a hanger with a crew room adjoining; the office had a small window where one could see the take-offs and landings. The airfield was a grass field and the runways were laid down to Somerfeld tracking and pegged to the ground. Somerfeld tracking was an ingenious form of fairly firm, pre-cast landing strip, a bit like a honeycomb, which could be rolled out onto a field to provide a runway in just a few hours. The company which made Somerfeld was, and still is, based here in Shropshire just outside Wellington.

The Flight Sergeant showed me into the office and introduced me to Flying Officer Lloyd. I gave him a smart salute whereupon he offered me a seat and welcomed me to the Squadron. "Would you like a cup of tea Cowling?" he enquired. "Yes please, Sir" I replied eagerly. "By the way, when you came in just now you saluted me," he said. "I've no time in this office for that rubbish. We have a job to do here, bullshit is completely unnecessary. Salute me outside of this office by all means, but you can still show respect laddie without bullshit!! Corporal, two mugs of hot tea please", he shouted. Then as an afterthought he added, "Oh! Do you take sugar?" "Yes please Sir. One", I said. "One with sugar Corp, please". "OK Sir, coming up", came a disembodied voice from the crew room, somewhere on the other side of the partition.

He explained that the Squadron consisted of 12 Fairey Battle light bombers. "I'll show you one when we've finished our tea break." A few minutes later we walked across the concrete apron to where the Battles were lined up. I climbed up inside and my first impression was that there was very little room to move but, I thought, I can get used to this, even though I knew that the Anson had far more room. After a little time to familiarise myself with the aircraft that I was to fly in, I went over to the stores to draw my flying kit. This kit would remain with me whilst I served in the RAF – however long or short that time might be. I was now kitted up and ready to go to war.

Fairey Battle bombers flying in formation - little more than oversized Spitfires but with less speed and fewer guns

The Fairey Battle was a single-engine, light bomber monoplane. It had a retractable under-carriage, a range of 1000 miles and a top speed of 241 mph. Cruising speed was about 200mph. The crew consisted of a pilot, a bomb-aimer/observer and a wireless operator/air gunner – that was me. The armaments were two guns, one fixed on the wing and the other amidships operated by the gunner.

Nevertheless, despite its lamentable lack of power, speed and weaponry, it was a Fairey Battle that shot down the first German aircraft of the Second World War on Wednesday 20th September 1939.

I made five operational flights on this aircraft, before they were withdrawn from front line service, but even at that I had beaten the odds for survival. Had I made any more I most certainly would not have lived long into 1940. The losses in this aircraft were frightening. The first mission I flew on, just a few days after arriving at RAF Duxford involved 71 Battles. Our mission was to fly across to France and try to stop the German advance towards the English Channel. The events which led to the disaster that was to become Dunkirk had started to unfold. The British ground troops of the BEF [the British Expeditionary Force] would be pushed back to the Channel; in a few weeks they would be squeezed into the pocket around Dunkirk. We lost 40 aircraft on that raid alone; 120 airmen shot down and the stark reality is that most of them would have been killed. The plane was hard enough to get out of when it was standing still on the ground, when it was full of smoke and fire and spinning towards the earth it would have been almost impossible in the few seconds available to the crew.

The problem was that the Fairey Battle was just no match for the German Messerschmitt Me109. The German fighter pilots had gained a lot of experience in the Spanish Civil War and knew how, with terrifying efficiency, to work together and shoot down large numbers of slow flying, lightly armed bombers. They simply treated us as target practice; they were like bees around a honey pot and we were the honey-coated cannon fodder. To make matters worse, these were all daytime raids which we carried out; we didn't have either darkness or fighter cover to protect us. We were totally exposed to the lethal 20mm cannons of the Messerschmitts.

I was not afraid to die but we were not even being given a fighting chance. The Battle was so underpowered and under armed that it was known as 'the flying coffin'. Nevertheless, I had survived my first bombing raid against the enemy and was no longer a rookie. It had been a baptism of fire, but there was worse to come; although it was just as well that at that time I didn't know it.

My last operational mission in a Battle was about 3 weeks later when 25 aircraft attacked a German target in northern France. We had found the target and had gone in in 3 waves. My own aircraft was in the first wave and we dropped our bombs pretty well on the spot. I was sitting behind the mid-ship guns, looking back over the target area to report the success of our run to the pilot, when I saw an Me 109 closing in on us very fast. Everything seemed to happen together then. I didn't have time to be frightened. I swung my guns round to bear on the incoming fighter, at the same time shouting, "109 skipper, 109 port side, corkscrew, corkscrew." Before the pilot could turn the Battle into a spinning nose-dive, I had the German in the spider's web of my gun sights. The Battle was vibrating heavily but I could clearly see the bright yellow nose cone swooping towards us. I squeezed the trigger with all my might and I saw my tracer bullets stretch out across the sky between us and rip into his fuselage, peppering the ugly black cross painted below the cockpit. At the same time the German pilot started firing at us and I could see the flashes from his wing-mounted cannons spitting certain death straight at me. Time seemed to pass in slow motion for those few seconds; there was no sound, no feeling, I was transfixed by the machine coming towards me, waiting for the searing pain as the hot metal entered my body. But the impact of my own machine gun bullets fired fractionally sooner, had been enough to spoil his aim and as the Battle began to turn and fall, the cannon shells flew by over our heads.

Instantly I was aware again; it was like opening the door to a noisy room. Our own engines were screaming and the Me109 roared passed with a thin trail of smoke in its slipstream. By now our skipper was corkscrewing the Battle for all our lives; a steep turn to port and then dive down at such a speed that the plane shuddered so violently I thought it would shake itself to bits. Over my shoulder I could see the ground rushing up at us and felt the 'G' force as the pilot struggled with the aircraft to bring it out of that dive. The ground was still getting nearer and the features of the French countryside were getting bigger and bigger. "Oh God," I whispered, "why me? This is it; we're not going to make it", and I thought of my mother and her tears. Then the aircraft started to respond. She was pulling up, we might make it. With little more than 100 feet to spare and with a scream that would have been the envy of any Stuka, the old Battle pulled level. I couldn't believe that she was going that fast, the ground flew past underneath me at a terrifying speed: but the skipper had done his job and we had lost our attacker. I am not sure whether I shot down that Me109 or just riddled it with bullets. I don't know what happened to the pilot; I saw no parachute and he might just as easily have been one of the explosions which were all around the target area; he may even have got back to his airfield. Quite honestly I didn't know and I didn't care. We were safe now and heading for home. Had I not fired my guns first, the German pilot would have shot us down and we would all have been killed. I did what I had been trained to do and this was war.

When Flying Officer Sam Reems landed us back at RAF Duxford we were one of only eight planes to return to base from the 25 that had taken off for that mission. Another 51 airmen had been lost that day. Another 51 husbands, sons, boyfriends; we knew them all in one way or another and the Airmen's Mess was becoming a very quiet place.

Messerschmitt bf109 fighter - the mainstay of the Luftwaffe Fighter Squadrons

Even to the 'brass hats' at the Air Ministry it had become clear that the Battle was wholly inadequate for a front line role and this last raid was the final straw. It was a simple matter of logistics. The Me109 pilots were shooting down the Battle's faster than we could train crews to fly them. We did not have enough trained aircrew to take these losses. The truth was we were running out of crews quicker than we were running out of aeroplanes. The Fairey Battle was withdrawn from front line service the next day. The aircraft still had an important role to play in the war but the Luftwaffe would no longer use it as target practice. Many were sent to Canada where they took part in training programmes and others were used to tow drogues for firing practice.

We were now stood down whilst those with 'scrambled egg' on their caps decided what we would fly next. During this time, the Flight Commander asked me what aircraft I would prefer to fly in. The chaps in the Mess had all heard what a marvellous aircraft the Sunderland Flying Boat was and even the media was allowed to say so, although this was actually for propaganda purposes after the losses of the Battle. I was not afraid of death but I was not prepared to be killed like a rat in a barrel and decided that I would be more useful to my King, my Country and the RAF if I was alive rather than dead and I put it to the CO in those terms. He must have been impressed because my request was approved and two days later I was posted to RAF Station Pembroke Dock on Sunderland Flying Boats.

Front gates Pembroke Dock - 210 Flying Boat Squadron HQ

Chapter 4
Coastal Command

By the time I had got from RAF Duxford down to London and across to Paddington Station, I was too late for a scheduled service to South Wales, so I hitched a ride on the milk train and I arrived at Pembroke Dock Railway Station early one frosty morning in 1940. I had my kit bag and my gas mask over my shoulder; I had been travelling for 15 hours; I was tired, hungry and despite wearing my greatcoat, I was bitterly cold. The wall to the docks on my right-hand side was about 15 to 20 feet high and the whole place resembled a prison. At the end of this wall were the imposing entrance gates, on each side of which stood an airman with fixed bayonet.

The Corporal of the guard directed me through a small side door and into the Guardroom, where I was brusquely confronted by the duty Sergeant who asked me for my identification form. Having inspected my papers and decided that I wasn't a threat to National security, he returned to his desk to telephone someone, somewhere to tell them that I had arrived. Duty Sergeant's are not noted for being kindly, however I must have got him on a good day because he allowed me to sit down on a bench to the right of the counter behind which he was sitting whilst I waited to be collected. In due course a Leading Aircraftman arrived and escorted me across the parade ground to my quarters. In the darkness of the early hours I could just make out the bulk of many large buildings, one of which turned out to be the Airmen's quarters, which would be my home for several months to come.

Airmen's Billets, Pembroke Dock

As it was still early morning and everyone was asleep, I placed my kit bag in the hall, had a quick rinse wash in the bathroom to freshen up and was shown the Airmen's Mess. I borrowed a mug and poured myself a tea from a large urn; milk and sugar were compulsory – they were already in the brew! I wasn't about to complain though as it was the most welcome mug of tea I had ever drunk. At the hatch to the kitchen I was handed a large bowl of porridge and on a plate a dollop of egg substitute, two slices of fatty bacon and cold toast. At my previous station, as an operational aircrew member, I would have had a choice of cereal, two fresh eggs, bacon, hot toast and a pot of tea. But then who was I to argue: I was still cold, hungry and thirsty. I hadn't eaten or had a drink of tea for 18 hours but most importantly, no one was going to put me into a flying coffin today.

It was 06.10 hours and I made my way back to my billet, the airmen's residential accommodation, where I met up with the Corporal who was in charge of the room. I retrieved my kitbag from the hallway and was shown a bed at the end of the room. Placing my belongings in the corner I met many of my future mates as they were getting up to start the day. Some were Riggers, others were Flight Engineers and the rest were WOP/AGs like me. A couple of these chaps could have been my dad, judging by their ages and were probably Regulars, but the others were youngsters of about my own age, 19 or 20. I was fit to drop and, pulling down my biscuits (3 mattresses) I made my bed, lay down and fell fast asleep.

Sunderland flying boat

Two hours later, having placed my belongings in the locker beside my bed, shaved, washed and smartened myself up, I reported to the Orderly Room, where else, and then carried on to the stores to collect my mug, spoon, knife and fork and after placing all these in my locker, I went over to the Flights. There I met the Flight Commander, Squadron Leader Pearce, an Officer who was clearly several years older than I was.

He was a pre-war pilot and was wearing his 'best blue' uniform, which I noticed was nearly turning green with age and was covered in small tiny holes. I thought that his quarters must be plagued with moths to make such a mess of his uniform. However I later found out that he always smoked a Sherlock Holmes pipe whilst flying and that after taking a breath in, he would blow out through the pipe, sending a fountain of lighted tobacco and ash into the cockpit, most of which landed on his uniform. Standing to attention and giving him a smart salute, I was welcomed with a good firm handshake. "Hello Cowling. I have an excellent report about you. I want you on my crew. You will be flying in Sunderland L2163. The lads are on board now. Flight, introduce Cowling to Corporal Smith and ask him to take him down to the dinghy."

The Corporal was a young, fair-haired fellow, about twenty-five years of age and he welcomed me to 210 Flying Boat Squadron. We jumped into the dinghy which was bobbing about on the water at the quayside and motored out across the harbour to where a very large four-engine flying boat was moored. Corporal Smith sat me in the front of the dinghy and so I had a good view of the great Sunderland slowly looming out of the winter mist which hung over the Dock. There was a slight breeze coming in off the sea and the salty spray coming over the front of the dinghy caught my face and stung my eyes. "Now I know why he sat me here", I thought. As we neared the flying boat a door in the side opened and the coxswain moved forward in the dinghy and with a boat hook on the end of a long pole, caught the Sunderland and drew us to the doorway. Ropes were not allowed on dinghies serving flying boats as there had once been a rather messy accident when the rope had become entangled in turning propeller blades! As the coxswain held the dinghy close to the Sunderland I jumped across the gap and was on board my first flying boat.

I was greeted by the crew of about eight members; Bill Miller introduced me to them all and explained he was the Rigger but was also in charge of the galley. They were just boiling up for a cup of coffee he said and invited me to join them. They were all such a friendly lot and made me feel very welcome right from the start. We sat on the galley bunk for about fifteen minutes and they wanted to know all about my background and how I came to be posted to 210 Squadron.

"Right," said Bill, "let me show you the boat." The mooring procedure was explained to me, that was part of the Rigger's job, and after going round with the WOP, Flight Engineer and Air Gunner and seeing the flight deck, I was seriously impressed at the size of the craft.

It was colossal; there was just no comparison with the Battle.

Browning guns

The Bolton Paul gun turret in the rear was all hydraulically controlled with four Browning .303 machine guns; the front turret was similar with two Brownings and each side of the mid-ship was a single Browning. I thought back to the old Battles I had just come from, with their less powerful Lewis machine guns and of how many lives could have been saved if they had been fitted with this sort of armoury. This was a formidably armed boat and I was impatient to fly in her.

Sunderland Flying Boats, which were fitted with four engines, were in operation throughout World War II. They had been adapted from the pre-war civilian passenger and mail flying boat, which had been used by Imperial Airways in particular, between the hundreds of small islands in the South Seas where a seaplane was an ideal form of transport. The flight capability of the Sunderland was about 3,000 miles and gave Coastal Command its first long distance aircraft. During the war its main task in Western Command was to escort convoys, and to search for and destroy U-boats, thus safeguarding the shipping lanes across the Atlantic Ocean which were so critical to Britain's survival.

As an island nation we could not survive long without

the imports of food, fuel and war materials which the Merchant Navy brought across the Atlantic, mainly from America. The Sunderlands were also used to reconnoitre fairly inaccessible places such as the Norwegian fjords, which because of their deep water were a favourite hiding place for German battleships. This was a very dangerous task as German fighters, such as the Me110 also patrolled above these fjords to prevent the ships being discovered and we lost many aircraft and friends on such ventures.

The day after my arrival I was awakened at 02.00 hours and, carrying my Irvine clothes [lamb's wool flying jacket] gas mask and wearing my lamb's wool flying boots and similar type of material trousers, climbed into the back of a 15cwt truck with the rest of the crew and was taken to the Airmen's Mess. There we enjoyed an early morning breakfast of cereal, fresh poached eggs and hot toast and the luxury of a mug of hot coffee. After breakfast we were driven to the jetty and boarded the dinghy which took us out to L2163. I'd learned my lesson though and this time I avoided sitting in the front of the dinghy. We slipped our moorings and took off into the night sky. We rendezvoused with a convoy in mid-Atlantic and escorted the 34 merchant ships, together with their Royal Navy escort to the safety of home waters. Altogether we were airborne for some 7 hours and the trip was entirely uneventful, I loved every minute of it.

I flew with this crew from 210 Squadron at Pembroke Docks on many such convoy patrols in the Western Approaches, the Bay of Biscay, the Shetlands Islands and the dangerous Norwegian waters. Our most popular meeting point with the enemy was over the Bay of Biscay where the Junker JU88's would come up from their bases in France to attack the convoys heading for Gibraltar and the Mediterranean.

The most famous of these convoys was what became known as the 'Malta Convoy'. The island was a British base and of vital strategic importance to the Allies in the Mediterranean. In 1941, the island was almost out of fuel and unable to defend itself. A relief convoy was put together including the great Texaco tanker, the *Ohio*. When the ship had been built in America, her plates had been welded instead of the traditional riveting. The Germans and Italians knew how important this convoy was to Malta and attacked it mercilessly all the way from Cape Finisterre to Malta harbour and although the *Ohio* was twice torpedoed, the welds held her together and she remained afloat long enough to deliver her valuable cargo. It was during this period that King George VI awarded the George Cross to Malta.

The JU88 was a two-engine, light bomber but it was fairly fast, very manoeuvrable and well armed for a bomber. It was the German's favourite weapon against British shipping after the submarine. The Mediterranean convoys were essential to keep our 8th Army, the Desert Rats, supplied in the battle for North Africa as they fought to keep Rommel from capturing Alexandria, Cairo and the Suez Canal. The fighting had swung back and forth through Libya and Tobruk had already swapped hands between the Germans and the British several times. The decisive battle of El Alamein, in which my brother Len was to take a front line part, was still more than a year away. The El Alamein campaign also produced the only bar to a VC of the Second World War and one of only three ever. In May 1941, 2nd Lieutenant Charles Hazlitt Upham won the VC on the island of Crete, by single handedly attacking a machine-gun nest and causing a withdrawal of German troops. A year later, now with the rank of Captain, Upham won the bar to his VC. Despite two serious wounds he led his men into battle, where he was further wounded when a machine-gun bullet broke his arm. Upham carried on and destroyed a tank and several machine-guns with grenades. Despite his injuries he survived the war and returned to his sheep farm on South Island, New Zealand.

The Germans knew that a decisive battle for North Africa was coming and did their best to sink as many ships as possible in a bid to sever the only supply line that the British had. But the German resources were stretched too and the Luftwaffe was still trying to recover from its losses in the Battle of Britain. The continued bombing of the British mainland was becoming a huge drain on the Luftwaffe bomber squadrons and in particular on their aircrews.

We had seen the Focke Wulf Fw 200 Condor long-range spotter plane shadowing the convoy for some time since the early morning sun had climbed into the eastern sky and we knew that it would have already given away the position of our ships to its French base. They would have radioed the convoy's size, position, speed and course, together with the three Corvettes and the Destroyer which made up the Royal Navy escort ships and our own presence in the sky above. We were too strong a force for a submarine attack, but an air attack was definitely an option to the enemy.

By midday the spotter plane had done its job and gone home. If we had been in the mid-Atlantic, a major change of course would have been an option for the convoy, but here in the Bay of Biscay there was nothing for it to do but to keep steaming south. We gained some more height and for another hour we stayed with the convoy, the steady rhythmic drone of the big Sunderland's engines providing an uneasy reassurance.

The afternoon wore on and then, far, far away in the distance we saw three tiny specks heading towards us. We didn't have to identify them; we knew that they would send JU88's, the Luftwaffe's fastest bombers, to attack the convoy. A Sunderland flying boat is not a Spitfire and we were not designed for aerial combat; this was now a job for the Royal Navy gunners. We got out of their way and climbed high up into the shifting banks of cumulo-nimbus clouds. Between breaks in the clouds however, we had a perfect view of the action below us as the skipper, Squadron Leader Pearce, his Sherlock Holmes pipe disgorging fountains of hot ash all over the cockpit banked round to keep the convoy in sight. As the JU88s neared the convoy, the three planes broke formation and made for the merchant ships in a gentle dive to drop their bombs. A hail of tracer fire streaked up from the escort ships towards them. The young pilot in the lead JU must have been hit, because it suddenly banked very sharply away from its run at the convoy. As the Hotchkiss ack ack guns on one of the Corvettes continued to fire, the bomber suddenly just blew up in the sky. It must have taken a direct hit on either the fuel tanks or the bomb load. Although I had seen many aircraft hit and go down in flames, I had never seen one explode in the air and the picture of that great ball of fire and smoke has remained with me to this day. I wasn't elated as I had expected to be, I think because I knew that, although we were at war, the crew were just airmen the same as us and now they were gone in an instant.

But the fight wasn't over and as we weaved in and out of the clouds I saw a second JU88 drop its bombs over one of the merchantmen. Two great fountain spouts of water erupted close to the ship's stern and the bomber peeled away from the convoy, but as it did so it turned right across the path of the Destroyer. Once more a great stream of tracer came up from the ship; the menacing black aircraft gave a sudden lurch in the sky and smoke and fire poured out of the starboard engine. It began to lose height and banked away and a few moments later one, then two then three little black sticks slipped from underneath it. The parachutes drifted down to the water and from my seat in the rear gun turret I could clearly see the airmen struggling to swim away from their 'chutes to avoid being smothered and drowned by the same silk which had just saved their lives.

But my eyes were drawn back to the stricken aeroplane which was falling away to the sea and in my headset I heard Bill whisper, "Get out man, for God's sake get out." But there was no fourth parachute; the Junkers crashed into the sea, cart-wheeled once, broke up and settled. In the space of a few seconds what was left of the plane slipped beneath the water, which from up here looked like frosted glass. The pilot had died ensuring that his crew at least had a chance of survival. That was the duty of every pilot and I regarded Squadron Leader

Pearce with wiser eyes after that episode.

It was all too much for the crew of the third bomber; we watched them ditch their bombs without any conviction harmlessly wide of the convoy and get to hell out of there and back to France to grieve the loss of their comrades. But I was just about to learn another hard lesson of war.

Satisfied that there were no other enemy aircraft around, we lost height and circled around the ships making sure that there was no U-boat attack poised to follow up the bombing raid. All the while I expected to see one of the ships down there stop and pick up the three surviving German airmen who had swum together and were bobbing about in the water. But one by one the ships steamed by and half an hour later we had moved on so far that I could no longer see the desperate, waving shapes in the sea.

Fairly soon our relief Sunderland came up to take over and we took our leave of the slow moving convoy and headed off to Gibraltar to refuel, eat and rest. In a quiet moment I asked Squadron Leader Pearce why none of the ships had stopped to pick up the three airmen. He gave me a fatherly smile and explained that it would take over a mile for even the smallest of the ships to stop; if they were close enough they could throw a scrambling net over the side, otherwise they would have to lower a boat, row to the airmen, pull them in, row back, lift the boat back on board, start the engines again and get back to full speed. All this would take an hour or more and meanwhile the convoy was steaming away from them. Whilst these three enemy airmen were being saved, the Captain would have put his ship, his cargo and the lives of his entire crew in mortal danger. These were home waters to the U-boats based in Brest and a British ship sitting motionless in the Bay of Biscay on a calm, hot summer afternoon was just begging to be torpedoed, either as it wallowed in the gentle swell or as it spent the next 12 hours trying to catch up the rest of the convoy. It just wasn't an option – and anyway, the crew of the third bomber knew where they were.

Haunted by the thought that one day that could be me, I didn't sleep much that night.

Two days later we returned to Pembroke Dock with a homebound convoy from South Africa, which we picked up out of Gibraltar off the Cape of Trafalgar. The return trip home was like so many similar flights, wholly uneventful with the tedium of the journey being broken only by the change of Watch and the meals which Bill rustled up in the galley.

One of the duties back at The Dock was to man the Strike Boat. This required a crew to remain on board their Sunderland for 24 hours at a time and be permanently ready for an urgent and immediate take-off. I can vividly remember the last night we were the Strike Boat; we sat in the relative calm of the Dock, listening to the lapping of the water against the hull of L2163. I had tuned the spare radio channel into the BBC Light Programme which was broadcasting the dance music of Carroll Gibbons and the Savoy Hotel Orpheans from London. Anne Lenner was singing "A Nightingale Sang in Berkley Square"; our boat felt very warm and cosy: the war seemed a far off event. As Anne Lenner was finishing this lovely song with "......I know 'cos I was there, that night in Berkley Square...." the balloon went up and shattered our peaceful evening. The air raid sirens sounded and we scrambled the boat ready for our take off orders. We could hear the unmistakable sound of German bombers coming in; they were flying low and fairly fast; almost certainly Heinkel He111s. From our position out in the Dock we had a grandstand view. The searchlights came on and the ack ack started; we could hear the whistle of the bombs as they neared the ground, then a series of loud 'crumps' followed by several huge explosions from the hill behind the town. We knew what they were going for and that they had hit their target. The oil tanks on the hill outside Pembroke were completely destroyed. The RAF station and town were hidden by dense black smoke for days as the oil fires burned themselves out.

All we could do was to sit and watch the attack unfold.

Pembroke Dock oil tanks on fire – John Evans Collection

Soon after this incident the Squadron was transferred en bloc to Oban, on the west coast of Scotland and No.209 Squadron replaced us at Pembroke Dock. Patrols from Oban continued up the Norwegian fjords, to Iceland and the mid-Atlantic. We were now much nearer the German U-boat lanes from Norway and the Baltic ports and this meant that we had longer in the air over their northern hunting grounds and routes of passage. This led to a lot more strikes on the U-boats and very many were sunk.

Chapter 5
Promotion and Sorties At Oban

It was now early 1941 and Bomber Command losses were mounting. We were still carrying out a lot of daytime raids and, other than the pilot, much of the aircrew were made up of Other Ranks i.e. not Officers and not NCOs [Non-Commissioned Officers]. News was filtering back to Britain from the French Resistance and from prisoners who managed to escape, that Other Ranks aircrew who survived a crash landing or had baled out of their burning aircraft and managed to land safely were, after capture by the Germans, being treated abominably in the prisoner of war camps. Many were kicked and severely interrogated for information which, at their rank, they just would not possess. Unsurprisingly the Gestapo were the most ruthless, but rank and file soldiers were also being ordered to disregard the Geneva Convention in their treatment of such aircrew.

To try to combat this ill-treatment, the Air Ministry based at Adastral House in London, decreed that all aircrew should immediately be promoted to the rank of Sergeant. Sergeants, as NCOs, were thus treated much more favourably than Other Ranks as POWs. So I became the proud owner of three stripes on each arm, my brass bullet was removed and replaced with a half wing over my left hand top pocket. We also had a pay rise, which would not have escaped the notice of the Air Ministry's civil servants. This was a big cost increase and gives some indication of just how serious a problem this had become for Other Ranks aircrew falling into enemy hands.

On a much lighter note, I remember very well the old time Sergeants in the Mess disapproving of us youngsters. They had served 20 years or more before their promotion to Sergeant and we young upstarts with only about two years' service were taking over their Mess. Due to the promotion of such a large number of aircrew on the Squadron all at the same time, we swamped their Mess. At the time I didn't appreciate their resentment but looking back we did upset their sense of status. To make things worse, two months later I was promoted to Flight Sergeant and I was now wearing a brass crown above my stripes. This rate of promotion would never have happened in peacetime of course, when these older regulars would have had to study and sit exams for their stripes. But we were at war and the whole Service had changed around. When crews took off, for some it was the last time and promotional vacancies came along very quickly – sadly, all too quickly.

However, I must have made an impression somehow with my Commanding Officer, because not long after my promotion to Flight Sergeant, when reading DRO's (Daily Routine Orders) I was pleasantly surprised to see that I had again been promoted, this time to Warrant Officer 1st class. This was a particularly good promotion for me because it meant that I could discard my thick cloth uniform which I had always found very uncomfortable and replace it with a light worsted uniform not unlike the ones the Commissioned Officers wore. I drew my new uniform from the stores and looked with pride at the cloth crown stitched onto the bottom of each of my sleeves. My father had been a Sergeant Major in World War 1 and it had taken him 22 years to reach that rank and here I was, a rank above him in only two years. My father, who had been in the Royal Army Medical Corps, had won the Military Medal on the Somme for saving the lives of wounded soldiers whilst under fire; little did either of us know that before the war was over I was to win the Distinguished Flying Cross, the RAF equivalent to his own medal.

So it was that I flew many sorties out over the Atlantic where convoy patrols were the stock in trade for the Sunderland crews. We were though only too painfully aware of the successes of the U-boats, which by now were hunting in the feared wolf packs on the merchant ships coming across the Atlantic. We knew that many survivors of these attacks would never be rescued and faced a long slow death in the open ocean. Torpedoes, fire, sinking ships, lifeboats and rafts loaded with survivors, often injured or covered in oil or both, floating amongst the debris which had once been their home; death did come quicker in winter because of the cold and the storms, but death it still was. These are the images which are forever etched in the memories of the crews who flew the Sunderland patrols. Memories which even now still haunt my nightmares.

I flew on many sorties with Flying Officer Reggie Baker, who earned the DFC flying in his favourite Sunderland P9624. It was when we were protecting a convoy of five ships and received a radio message that a merchant ship had been torpedoed; we were ordered to search for the attacker. Another Sunderland spotted the conning tower of U-51 cutting through the water and dropped a depth charge over the target. The sea erupted in a great white plume and U-51 was brought to the surface. We dived down low over the sub and dropped four anti-submarine bombs right along its length. The U-boat was doomed from the moment Reggie Baker lined up the big Sunderland and released the bombs. Below us amongst the boiling water, we saw the gush of oil coming to the surface as U-51 and her crew slipped beneath the waves to join the merchant ship she had sunk just half an hour earlier. Its hunting days were over.

On another trip we received a Morse Code message to say that the 11,000-ton liner, the *City of Bernares*, had been torpedoed notwithstanding that it was clearly a passenger ship. We flew to the area where the sinking had taken place and found a lifeboat containing 40 adults and six children, the only survivors from the stricken ship. On this occasion, being as sure as we could that the U-boat which had sunk the liner was long gone, we guided a Royal Navy Destroyer to the lifeboat and the survivors, at considerable risk to the Destroyer and its crew, were rescued.

Flight Lieutenant Van de Kiste was another very experienced pre-war pilot and I flew with him on several successful missions. One afternoon whilst on patrol we spotted a periscope slicing through the surface of the sea below us, looking for the convoy we were protecting. This was an attack for us to carry out. The periscope meant that the U-boat was just beneath the surface and that it was vulnerable to attack by depth charges. We made our run in and dropped two charges set to go off at a very shallow depth. Sure enough, as the eruption in the sea died down it was followed by a large bubble of air and then, as we climbed up away from the tormented water, we could clearly pick out a slick of oil spreading out over the surface of the sea for more than a mile. A definite kill.

Helplessly watching merchant ships being torpedoed and sunk, sailors on fire jumping into the sea or burning to death in a patch of flaming oil, drowning before our very eyes and bodies floating on the water were just part of what had become our lives on 210 Flying Boat Squadron. From time to time we had the success of sinking a U-boat and mightily excited about it we were too. Every U-boat sunk was one less to attack our convoys and kill the sailors who were risking their lives each day to bring the vital war materials to the ports of Britain. At this time, in 1941, America had not entered the war even though President Roosevelt was giving as much help as he could without actually declaring war on Germany. The result was that after the fall of France in May 1940, Britain and the Empire stood alone against Germany. We had won the Battle of Britain through the courage of the fighter pilots. Our job was to make sure that the courage of our merchant seamen wasn't in vain and that we won the Battle of the Atlantic too. Making our shots count was very important and we never lost sight of the fact that the enemy felt just the same.

Lt. Commander Otto Kretschmer, born in 1912, became Germany's top U-boat ace, commanding U-23 and then U-99. He sank 44 allied ships, a total of 250,000 tonnes and too many lives in the first 18 months of the war. He operated at night, on the surface and fired a single torpedo at point blank range, usually preying on lone ships. U-99 was eventually sunk but sadly not by us and he was taken prisoner in March 1941 whilst attacking convoy HX112. Kretschmer survived the war as a prisoner in Yorkshire and then Canada and went on to rebuild the navy of post war Germany, reaching the rank of Admiral.

One night we took off from Oban with a crew of ten. The weather was atrocious, as it can be at any time of year along the west coast of Scotland. Our mission was to meet up, in mid-Atlantic, with a convoy of 43 merchant ships and their Royal Navy escort and shadow them back to home waters. Days later the Royal Navy would escort them into the Clyde between the mainland and the Mull of Kintyre and onto the port of Glasgow.

The cloud base was only 200 feet and so for three hours we flew by dead reckoning to our rendezvous point. Whether by good luck or brilliant navigation and flying by Squadron Leader Pearce, out of the cloud we met up with the convoy in the middle of a 3,000-mile ocean. I shall never forget that wonderful sight of all those ships steaming across the Atlantic exactly where they should have been and at the right time. We fired our Verey pistol flare to identify ourselves with the colour of the day. The Captain of the lead Destroyer was thankfully working from the same set of Orders and acknowledged us. His other choice was to blow us out of the sky! But just as we were congratulating ourselves on our navigation skills, at that very moment there was a shout through the intercom, "Tallyho, Tallyho. Torpedo port bow". The Sunderland's klaxon horn sounded, filling the boat with a deafening noise. All the crew jumped to Action Stations and there, plain to see just below the surface was the telltale streaming wake of a torpedo skimming through the water and heading straight for a ship in the convoy. We dived down to 30 feet off the ocean surface and the port mid gunner fired his .303 Browning machine guns at the deadly tube. He filled the torpedo with bullets but nothing would deter it from its course; there was no more we could do but to watch helplessly and circle the doomed ship.

The two closest Destroyers fanned out and raced to the area, using their Sonar to track the U-boat, which by now had long since dived well out of our visibility range. We stayed with the merchant ship and left the sub to the Royal Navy. Meanwhile I had with me, ironically, a German Leica camera and took a series of photographs of the events as they unfolded below. The first photograph was taken with the torpedo entering the doomed ship as we continued to circle. The series of photographs which I took show the merchant ship slowly sinking to the bottom of the ocean, survivors in the water, climbing into their lifeboat, raising their sail and my last photograph shows them in their boat. (see page 59)

Then the Navy must have got a contact because all hell was let loose down there. A Corvette had now joined the two Destroyers and the three ships criss-crossed the area and laid a pattern of depth charges in the position where they clearly thought the U-boat was skulking beneath the waves. The explosions were breath taking, with spouts of sea water extending some 30 feet into the air: but no kill this time.

We carried out a square search of the area for another one and half hours, flying at only 100 feet above the waves. We really wanted that U-boat, but it had slipped away. Returning to the convoy we signalled the Captain of the lead Destroyer on our Aldis lamp that we would land and pick up the survivors. We knew that the ships in the convoy would not stop for them, particularly since we had not been able to find and destroy the U-boat. It would just be too dangerous for anyone to stop out there. Because the sea was fairly choppy we needed to lighten the aircraft and so we dumped everything we could into the sea; our 8 x 250lb bombs, all our guns, ammunition and other heavy equipment all went overboard as we approached the surface of the sea to land. Just as our hull touched the water, a huge wave, about 20 feet high, hit our port float and just about ripped it off. It was completely destroyed and hung helplessly from the mainplane by two strands of wire. With tobacco erupting from the pipe in his mouth like Mount Vesuvius, Pearce gave the four great engines of the Sunderland full throttle; the noise was deafening, even inside the aircraft. The lumbering bulk of the Sunderland just clipped the wave tops as she slowly lifted into the darkening sky, but we were airborne again and heading for base. We all knew that we were very lucky not to have joined the sailors in their lifeboat – but at least we had tried.

The poor unfortunate survivors were left to their own resources. We had tried but couldn't manage to save them. We couldn't land on the water now even if we wanted to; we would tip right over and that prospect still awaited us when we tried to land at Oban. Our own troubles were far from over: in the event we landed in the bay at the edge of the Base and slid up onto the sandy beach, writing off the other float and twisting our propellers. The sudden jar of the boat on the beach threw us all along the inside of the fuselage and about half the crew ended up with broken arms and legs. I was lucky and escaped with just a couple of bruises, but whatever our injuries were, we were more fortunate than those poor souls whom we had had to leave behind in that open lifeboat on the sea.

The torpedo has struck just forward of the funnel

The merchant ship starting to settle in the water

Her decks are now awash as the crew take to their lifeboat; some crew are already in the water

She has broken her back and the bow section slips away . . .

. . . followed by her stern

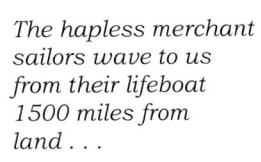

The hapless merchant sailors wave to us from their lifeboat 1500 miles from land . . .

Soon after this incident I was sent back to Gunnery School for the advanced course where I qualified as a Gunnery Leader. This was an important designation because it gave me the authority to control the fire of the gunners when attacked by enemy aircraft and I could instruct the pilot, who would sometimes be a Commissioned Officer and so senior in rank to me, to manoeuvre the aircraft as I thought fit in order to avoid the enemy or conversely, into a more favourable position for the gunners to engage the enemy. Essentially the job was that of attack and defence co-ordinator in the aircraft during any hostile action and to work properly a good understanding and relationship with the pilot was needed.

Not long after I returned from Gunnery School we were ordered to fly up to Invergordon on the northeast coast of Scotland, not far south of Wick. Whisky connoisseurs better know Invergordon as the home of Scotland's only single *grain* whisky. We had flown to Invergordon in Sunderland L5798 and were on detachment with two other boats. Our orders were to find the German troopships thought to be hiding in Hardangerfjorden and what a trip it turned out to be. We had flown to the fjords before and so we knew how dangerous it was going to be. Our route was to take us more or less in a straight line due east across the North Sea [allowing for the curvature of the earth] to Haugesund, which lies about 50 miles north of Stravanger. From there we would turn north and search amongst the many fjords which make up the major fjord complex of Hardangerfjorden, and see if we could locate the troopships.

We took off in the very early hours one morning in fairly settled weather but just off the Norwegian coast we flew into a really heavy snowstorm which made navigation to Hardangerfjorden difficult. Still, we consoled ourselves with the thought that the weather was so bad it would almost certainly keep the Luftwaffe on the ground. That consolation didn't last long though because as we got over Haugesund, we ran into very heavy anti-aircraft fire. We took a hit to our starboard mid-fuel tank and the main hull, but despite this damage we pressed on to our objective. As we flew over Garvin we again encountered very severe flak which tried to finish us off by piercing our port side mid-fuel tank and making a mess of our tail plane.

At this stage of the war Sunderland fuel tanks were not self-sealing and we were now losing fuel at a critical rate. If we didn't do something about it, not only wouldn't we have any chance of accomplishing our mission, we wouldn't have any chance of getting home either. If we didn't die in the freezing waters of the North Sea, where the average survival time was about 30 seconds, a prison camp beckoned. Neither prospect was inviting. What we needed to do was to plug those holes in one of the fuel tanks and we had the equipment on board to do it – chewing gum. Flight Sergeant Derrick Buley was the smallest member of the crew and so he volunteered to crawl deep into the wing cavity and plug the leaking fuel tank holes with chewing gum. Derrick crawled right into the wing whilst I followed him in and lay in the wing between him and the rest of the crew, who madly chewed gum for all their worth to keep us supplied. We could certainly have shown a few of today's football managers how to chew gum in a crisis! When we got back to Invergordon, the fitters pumped more than 400 gallons of high-octane fuel out of the bilges; more than enough to have blown us all sky-high. Derrick was awarded the Distinguished Flying Medal for his actions that night.

Flight Sergeant Derrick Buley, DFM

Some of our operational missions were undoubtedly easy to the extent that we did not encounter the enemy, but 12 or 14 hours of continuous flying brings it own problems and too many simple but sometimes fatal mistakes borne out of tedium and fatigue resulted. Other trips, like the Hardangerfjorden mission were difficult and dangerous. But for all that the boys in Bomber Command thought that we were all on holiday and maybe they were right because they were losing so many crews every day and night in bombing raids over Germany.

During April 1941, 210 Squadron took delivery of the new Catalina Flying Boat. This was an American two-engine flying boat with a longer range than a Sunderland. In fact with overload tanks a Catalina could stay airborne non-stop for a staggering 33 hours. This was going to prove to be an invaluable asset later on. The 1st to the 19th of April was set aside for crew conversion as we started to re-equip with the new Catalinas and on the 19th April I flew as Gunnery Leader with Curley Wheeler on our first operational trip in Catalina AH539.

As the weather improved and the days got longer we

The PBY Catalina flying boat

continued with our escort duties to the mid-Atlantic and to the Arctic. With the lengthening summer days the longer flying time of the Catalina was proving very important. It meant that crews did not have to turn round so often and could stay and hunt for a U-boat at an attack location for much longer than the U-boat could stay under the sea. The Type V11B U-boat, the Sea Wolf, which was the mainstay of the U-boat fleet, could stay submerged for about 18 hours, whereas the Catalina could stay in the air for 33 hours. It started to count.

After some of these escort missions we would often land in Iceland and return the next day to either Sullom Voe in the Shetland Islands, or to Oban. Now and again on these trips we landed on Lough Erne near Enniskillen in Northern Ireland to wash out our boat with fresh water. On these occasions a couple of us would blow-up one of our rubber dinghies and paddle ashore to buy eggs and butter from the nearby farms, but the local Irish people were very friendly and kind and would not accept any money, giving us as much as they could. Once back at our base we would share our goodies with all the crews. It is difficult to convey today what a real treat it was to have fresh eggs and butter – and these eggs had often been laid just a few hours before we were eating them. No wonder we were so grateful for them.

Chapter 6
His Majesty's Commission

The west coast of Scotland can produce some of the finest weather in Europe as well as some of the worst. On that Monday morning in June 1941, the day dawned with the wonderfully quiet, peaceful glow which always heralds a beautiful summer day. As I stepped out of the Mess and looked across the bay, the sea was like a sheet of glass. It mirrored the surrounding hills and reflected the azure blue of the early morning sky; the lapping of the water on the shore was barely audible. It was going to be a scorcher and it felt so good to be alive. I took a moment to think of the boys who would die on this beautiful June day... and then turned to get on with my job.

At 09.30 hours I was called before the Group Captain at Dungallen House, our Headquarters at Oban. Oh God, what now. My mind raced over the events of the last few days and our last mission in particular to think of anything which had gone so seriously wrong as to be summoned to Groupie's office. I knocked on his door and waited for the authoritative "Come in". "Ah, Cowling, thank you for coming over. I've been reviewing your Service record and have decided to recommend you for a Commission. You'll travel to London to be interviewed on Thursday. Good luck. You deserve this." I was so taken aback I nearly forgot to say, "Thank you, Sir". I saluted the Group Captain and left his office in a daze. Outside Dungallen House the birds were singing in the rhododendron bushes, which were just awash with colour. I hadn't even noticed them on the way in but now they were part of a perfect day.

That evening I packed my kit ready for the trip south and early next morning, with a railway warrant in my pocket I boarded the slow train from Oban to Glasgow. All the trains from Oban to Glasgow were slow: they still are. It is single track for most of the way with passing places at each of the many stations. The railway was the lifeblood of these small communities at this time. Then as now, a train is only allowed along a section of the track if the driver has the tally in his cab. That way, uncomfortable head-on collisions are avoided, but it makes for a slow journey. I didn't mind though on this occasion. The scenery is just magnificent along this route and the weather was so lovely. The railway line follows the glen around the top of Loch Awe, the longest loch in Scotland, and the backdrop is the Cruachan massif, at the heart of which lies Ben Cruachan itself; a mysterious mountain forever connected with the missing Roman Ninth Legion which marched out of York around AD 120 to quell the troublesome Caledonians and was never seen again. All 4,000 Roman soldiers who left York that day simply disappeared but the Standard of the Ninth Legion, bearing the solid gold eagle, is fabled to have turned up on Ben Cruachan.

I reached Glasgow Queen Street Station by late morning and, in need of directions, found a born and bred Glaswegian porter. I asked him from which platform I could get the train to Shrewsbury. His accent bore no resemblence to the English language that I knew and I couldn't understand a single word he said to me, which must have been obvious to him because he just shrugged his shoulders and pointed to the information office near the entrance. I tried again with the elderly clerk behind the half screen, but this time showed him my travel warrant. "Och, you'll be wanting St. Enoch, son. It's the other side of toon. The No.8 tram'll tak yous there. It stops reet ootside the front dor." Back out in the sunshine, standing on the pavement in George Street, the city was buzzing. This was a time of great transition from horse drawn to motorised transport and they were both filling the streets as they went about their business. I had heard the old clerk correctly, the tram stop was right there in front of me. As I stood waiting I just hoped no one else would speak to me. A few minutes later the green and cream tram came clanking around the corner, its wheels gripping the rails which were laid like sinews between the black granite setts, and the salmon with the gold ring in its mouth, the City of Glasgow's Coat of

Arms, gleaming on its side.

The 'clippie' was a nice looking girl of about 17, whose body seemed to have been squeezed into someone else's Glasgow City Corporation uniform. The effect though was rather appealing to a young serviceman. I asked her for a single ticket to St. Enoch station, but I pronounced it St. Eunuch much to her amusement. I paid her the 1½d fare, told her that I hadn't been to Glasgow before and would she tell me when I got to the right stop. She smiled and chatted away to me in between taking other fares on the short journey but I understood little of what she said, although as we neared the stop she bent forward and said quietly, "We's here just noo. Here's the stop for yous." And then with a serious look, she gently touched my arm and said, "You mind you tak care o' yoursen," and then added with a twinkling smile as I got off her tram, "an' come back te see me soon. Promise noo". I returned her smile and called back from the pavement, "I promise" and as she pressed the button twice the bell rang above the driver's head and the tram whirred away taking her out of my life. I was rather touched though by her concern and impressed by the friendly city I had never been to before.

I suppose she didn't see that many aircrew in Glasgow and most, like me, would just be passing through. Most of the Service personnel would be sailors from the many warships whose base this was, or soldiers from the local Regiments. Glasgow was very heavily bombed during the war. The area was an important target for the Germans; it was a major industrial centre and army training base particularly for the Royal Artillary; it had the commercial docks and the Naval bases along the Clyde, but most of all it was the home of the great shipbuilding yards of Fairfields, MacIntire's, Burrell's and John Brown's, which had built the famous RMS *Queen Mary* launched on 26 September 1934 and RMS *Queen Elizabeth* in 1938; now they were all building warships. A few weeks before, in March 1941, there had been a series of particularly heavy raids which had devastated Clydeside, including Henderson's, Denny's of Dumbarton and the world

Henderson's, Denny's of Dumbarton and the world famous Singer factory at Singer, a suburb which still takes its name from the sewing machine company.

I looked up at the beautiful façade of St. Enoch Station, a building which sadly no longer exists. As well as being a mainline terminus station for the LMS, St. Enoch was, and indeed still is one of the stops on the Glasgow underground, even though the great station building has gone. This was the first underground railway system in the world and is a circle line passing under the River Clyde twice as it links north and south Glasgow. As I stood there admiring the building I thought about my days as a pupil architect in Shrewsbury. Those days seemed a lifetime away; I could never have dreamt then that in just two years time I would be going to London to be interviewed for His Majesty's Commission. What would old Arthur Williams say, and smiled to myself as I thought of him at his drawing board in Dogpole.

I walked through the Gothic portals of the station and joined all the other Service men and women looking for the right southbound train. I knew that I would need to change at Carlisle and Crewe before getting to Shrewsbury. Carlisle 12.35, platform 7. That will do nicely. It will give me time to get a cup of tea and a sandwich from the WVS trolley and then find a seat. The great station was a cauldron of noise, with smoke and steam hissing from the powerful long distance passenger locomotives and the local tank engines alike; whistles blowing, people talking and as always, a Sergeant or two barking orders at their unfortunate charges.

Surprisingly for wartime Britain, the train left St. Enoch Station more or less on time and after a brief stop at Kilmarnock, we travelled on over the Southern Uplands and down the lovely valley of the River Nith to Dumfries where Robert Burns had spent the last years of his life. We waited at Dumfries for a short time to meet the local boat train connection from Stranraer and then carried on to Carlisle. My train to Crewe was waiting and a short time later we were on our way again, through Penrith the county town of Westmoreland as it was then and on to Lancaster, Preston and Crewe.

By now it was 19.00 hours and I was glad I had had that sandwich from the WVS trolley because I was getting hungry but was looking forward to tasting my mum's cooking for the first time in 18 months. Crewe was as chaotic as always but eventually the slow stopping train to Shrewsbury pulled in and we all joined the other passengers. There was no chance of a seat this time so I just stood in the corridor along with everyone else and watched between the trails of engine smoke as the familiar Cheshire and Shropshire countryside drifted by in the evening light. Soon enough I recognised the outskirts of the town and felt the train slow as we pulled into the splendid GWR station. It felt really good to be home again.

Mum and dad were at the station to meet me and had brought the car, a real luxury then: and a meal on the table when I got in. I stayed overnight with my parents and the next day I caught the mid-morning train down to London where I stayed in the Regent Hotel in Piccadilly.

The blackout was total and I didn't think there was any point in wandering about in the darkness of London. Nevertheless, I'd certainly picked the right time to visit London. The last concerted night raid here was on May 10 1941, exactly a year to the day that Neville Chamberlain had resigned and Winston Churchill had become Prime Minister. That day was one of very mixed fortunes for the Germans. Certainly the House of Commons had been damaged in the raid but that same night Rudolf Hess, Hitler's deputy, had parachuted into Eaglesham just south of Glasgow, was arrested by a local 'bobby' and spent the rest of his life in jail, mostly at Spandau Prison in Berlin. Also that night the Luftwaffe had lost 14 aircraft in the London raid alone, shot down by RAF Beaufighters including one flown by Flight Lieutenant John 'Cats-eyes' Cunningham from No.604 Squadron who, as a night fighter pilot, shot down 15 enemy aircraft in just 10 months during 1940-41. The Luftwaffe had not been back to London since. The Beaufighter, which was armed with four cannon, six machine guns and radar proved too much for the Germans; they had more or less given up on London because their losses were too high and Britain wasn't weakening. Hitler needed the aircraft for Operation 'Barbarossa', the attack on the USSR and so stopped the bombing raids. But it wasn't all one way; just two weeks after that costly raid the German battleship Bismark sank the pride of the British Navy HMS *Hood*, with the loss of all but three sailors – she just blew apart.

I stayed in the hotel and had a couple of quiet drinks in the bar. The wireless was playing Henry Hall and his Orchestra and the relaxed mood suited me: I needed to be up early the next day, it was Thursday. My appointment at Adastral House was at 10.00 hours and I didn't want a thick head. Looking very smart in my new best blue and with an extra dollop of brylcreem on my hair, I stepped into a taxi outside the hotel at 09.15 hours and was driven to the front door of the Royal Air Force Headquarters. I gave the taxi driver a tip of more money than I could really afford and walked into the magnificent marble entrance hall of Adastral House. I gazed around me like a country boy looking at the big city lights. I remember thinking that this is where Air Chief Marshall Dowding, the architect of the Battle of Britain victory, walked every day.

The elderly Commissionaire, proudly wearing his World War 1 medals and having enquired of my business at Adastral House, ushered me to a nearby waiting room. I was 21 years of age and had been on active service for over 18 months; I had been shot at by the enemy and seen things I would rather not have seen but still my knees were knocking and my heart was pounding at the thought of what lay ahead of me. Suddenly the door opened and a very attractive shapely WAAF Officer came in and verified my name. She smiled at me and asked me to follow her. We walked along the lofty deserted tiled passageway to a lift, the steel tips on her shoes echoing to her perfect step in the silence of the long corridor.

Inside the lift, which creaked and groaned as it took us up to the first floor, my hands were sweating and my heart was beating so loudly that I was sure she would be able to hear it. The lift stopped and the young WAAF Officer slid open the concertinaed iron gate, stepped out onto the polished wooden landing and led the way to an imposing oak panel door. She smiled at me again and gently put her hand on my shoulder, "Just relax", she said in her very English Rodean accent, "I'm sure you will be all right".

With her delicate knuckles she tapped on the door and held it open for me as I went in. I took two steps forward, stood to attention and gave my smartest salute. At the far end of the room behind a polished table the size of a snooker table, sat an Air Vice Marshall with, on his left, an Air Commodore complete with fighter pilot's moustache and to his right, a much younger Group Captain. The Air Vice Marshall invited me to remove my cap and to sit down on the chair right in front of him. He obviously had my service record in front of him and remarked that I was a brave young man as he briefly recounted some of my more hair-raising missions. I had never thought of myself as being brave, simply doing my job, and it settled me down a bit. During the next half an hour I was asked a wide range of questions by all three of them.

What a relief it was when at last I was thanked for attending and told to go home for seven days leave. I stood up, replaced my cap, saluted, and with my head swimming stepped out into the cool of the passageway. The pretty WAAF Officer was there waiting to escort me back to the marble hall. She flashed me that lovely smile again and said, "I'm sure they were very pleased with you. Are you going back home to Shrewsbury for your leave?" I said that I was. By now we had retraced our steps to the marble hall and as she turned to me and said, "Well, goodbye and do enjoy your leave at home", she reminded me of Celia Johnson. I hailed a taxi to Paddington Station and seven hours later I was sitting at home in Shrewsbury telling my parents of my experience with the interview panel. My father nodded sagely whilst my mother simply glowed with pride.

Two days later I received a telegram at home from my Squadron Adjutant congratulating me on attaining my Commission. I was given a further seven days leave with instructions to purchase my Officer's uniform locally. I was now a Pilot Officer.

Commissioned - Pilot Officer E.A. Cowling, 11th June 1941

At the end of my leave I retraced my train journey and returned to 210 Squadron Base at Oban – only now I wore my Officer's uniform. When I arrived, my old mates with whom I had flown for over 12 months, all lined up to meet me off the train. As I walked along the platform they stood to attention and saluted me; I was so embarrassed and self-conscious. Of course the NCOs' Mess was now out of bounds to me except in an official capacity and so I had to pluck up the courage and walk into the Officers' Mess. Most of the Officers were unaware of where I had been for the last fortnight and just stared at me. Only 14 days ago I had had to stand to attention, salute and call them 'Sir'. God, I thought, this is worse than my interview in London. Suddenly Flight Lieutenant Mac McKinley, [he was actually christened David Cecil

McKinley, but we all knew him as Mac] who had been my Skipper on a few missions, walked across to me, shook my hand and congratulated me on my promotion. He bought me a beer and introduced me to the Officers who were standing around in the group. The ice was broken and I was accepted into the Mess. Little could I have conceived then that McKinley and I would soon be sent on one of the most important and subsequently historic missions of the Second World War.

For the month before my promotion I had been flying with Warrant Officer Curly Wheeler. He would give me at least 20 years; he was an excellent pilot and we had spent many flying hours surveying parts of the Arctic looking for a German radio station which Intelligence had told us had been installed there. This work was really very interesting but since I now held the rank of Pilot Officer and Curley and the rest of the crew were all Non-Commissioned Officers I was required to leave the crew. I was rather disappointed as I had enjoyed those missions.

Inevitably, as a junior Commissioned Officer on the Squadron, it was not all glitz. I was the one usually chosen to do the routine jobs; sent to a deceased airman's home to support the family at his funeral; Officer-in-Charge of the Funeral Party or Duty Officer. This latter task meant entering the Airmen's Mess, generally with Flight Sergeant Palmer, who was a grey haired Regular coming to the end of his service. He would shout out, "Any complaints for the Officer?", much to the raucous laughter of my former Mess companions. But I was learning fast.

Chapter 7

From The White House ......

On Saturday 26th July 1941, together with four other handpicked aircrew, I was ordered to be at Dungallen House at 11.00 hours to see the Commanding Officer. Among that team were Derrick Buley, the young Flight Sergeant WOP/AG who had so diligently patched up the holes in our Sunderland's fuel tanks as we desperately chewed chewing gum over the coast of Norway and Bill Miller, who had first welcomed me aboard Sunderland L2163 back in Pembroke Dock.

By 10.55 we had all arrived at Dungallen House and, looking around at the assembled company, we knew that something unusual was in the air. We were all drawn from various crews and that meant a special job and almost certainly a dangerous one. After a few minutes we were shown into the CO's office. We saluted, were asked to sit down and a young WAAF brought us all a cup of tea. This was going to be big; tea with the CO was almost unheard of. He thanked us for coming and told us that the meeting was top secret and should not be mentioned around the Squadron. He then said, "I want you all to write a letter home to your next-of-kin telling them you will be out of the country for a short time but will contact them on your return", and then handed a sheet of notepaper and an envelope to each of us. Since I was single, I wrote to my mother. We were told not to seal the envelopes so that the Censor could ensure that we had written home in the terms we had been instructed to.

The CO apologised that he could not tell us anything further at this juncture, but we should all be honoured that we had been selected for this most important forthcoming trip. He considered us to be the most experienced members of the Squadron and that was why we had been chosen. He shook hands with each of us in turn and we left Dungallen House. Well that and the letter home, just about sealed it for us; this mission was going to be so dangerous that there was a pretty good chance that we were not going to come back from it.

The following day, the 27th July Flight Lieutenant Mac McKinley and Pilot Officer Owen, with a crew of six and four passengers had flown to Loch Lomond, one of Scotland's most beautiful loch's, where the 'bonnie, bonnie banks' are covered with wild flowers and the high mountains of Ben Lomond and Ben Vorlich sweep down to its shores. They were there for crew training and to give the boat a complete wash out in fresh water, in the same way we had done on Lough Erne in Northern Ireland.

It was a warm Sunday afternoon and the crew were enjoying the tranquillity of their surroundings. A few people had come out from Glasgow as they had done for decades, in charabancs, on bicycles, and a wealthy few from Milnegavie, by car. No matter how they had come, they were all there to escape the devastation, debris and destruction of the city; to enjoy the clean fresh air and the peaceful setting of the loch that is mentioned in more Scottish songs than any other. The water was as smooth as a mill pond and Ben Lomond produced a mirror image on the surface. A few children played at the water's edge on the headland at Sloy, near to where the hydroelectric power station now stands, as their parents watched on, glad of the momentary break from the war.

Out of the clear blue sky of that lazy Sunday afternoon, an RAF Catalina flew over the loch and circled McKinley's craft, signalling on the Aldis lamp. McKinley was ordered to return to base immediately. He reported to the CO and was told that the next day he was to fly to the base at Invergordon for an urgent and secret mission.

When McKinley's Catalina, W8416, landed back at Oban from Loch Lomond later that afternoon, Bill Miller, Derrick Buley, myself and the other two of the selected crew, were instructed to go on board for the night and to prepare the boat for the long journey. Long-range tanks were fitted in the hull and we knew that wherever it was that we were bound, it was going to be a long way there and back. We prepared an evening meal and after ensuring that the boat was secure, we settled down on the bunks in our sleeping bags for the night. As I drifted off to sleep, I couldn't help wondering what this was all about, where our mission would take us and whether any of us would ever see Oban again.

David McKinley on the steps of 'Aries' 26th May 1945 at RAF Shawbury, Shropshire

The following day dawned bright and cheerful, but we

were preoccupied with the mission which lay ahead of us and which at that stage none of us had any idea about what it entailed. McKinley, who was to be our Skipper for the trip and his co-pilot, Pilot Officer Owen came on board. The Rigger put the boat on short moorings and we were soon taking off for a quick trip of 30 minutes to give us a chance to test the automatic pilot. On these sorts of flights lasting 20 and 30 hours, the automatic pilot was invaluable to give the human pilots a break from the controls. The test went well and we landed and returned to moorings.

We were met by a supply dinghy which was loaded up with boxes full of food and a countless number of large thermos flasks. Bill, our Rigger, took control of everything since he was always the chef in the galley, in addition to his many other duties. Because of the additional fuel on board in the long-range tanks, which was high octane and highly inflammable and which had to be hand pumped into the main fuel tanks when needed, it was absolutely imperative that no naked flames were to be used on board. On this trip we would not be able to light the primus stoves and so the only hot meals we would get would be out of the thermos flasks.

On a previous mission McKinley had been flying with a mixed American and Canadian crew and high above the Atlantic, had smelt aviation fuel and tobacco smoke. He went aft only to discover the American engineer transferring fuel via the hand pump to open fuel tanks with a lighted cigar in his mouth, seemingly oblivious to the danger he had created. Seizing the airman's cigar, McKinley threw it out of a porthole and then summoned his very young Canadian co-pilot. Handing his pistol to the Canadian he said, "If the Engineer moves, shoot him, and shoot to kill." Having fuel sloshing about in an aircraft is a risky business.

When we were satisfied that the boat was ready to go, we taxied out from our inshore mooring and took off as we had done so many times before. Looking out of one of the starboard portholes as McKinley banked the big aircraft round to the northeast, I could see Oban receding behind us. A small collection of buildings huddled around the bay with John McCaig's Tower, in the form of the Coliseum in Rome, standing out clearly on the hilltop overlooking the town. McCaig, a wealthy local businessman had built this folly as a memorial to his family. Below us the next Atlantic convoy was being put together and the ships were anchored in the Firth of Lorn, which leads into Loch Linnie and on up to Fort William.

The flight to Invergordon lasted for an hour and a quarter, during which time the Skipper contacted us all on R/T. We landed on the calm waters of the bay at Invergordon and went on short moorings. As McKinley had promised over the R/T on the journey in, we were now to be fully briefed on our mission. We were told that we would be flying four important passengers from Invergordon to the Arctic port of Archangel in Russia. It was 28th July 1941 and barely five weeks since the Germans had invaded Russia in the biggest invasion that country had ever experienced.

The whole purpose of the journey was to take US President Roosevelt's special envoy, a 50-year-old American politician named Harry Hopkins, to Russia to meet Stalin. Churchill had personally made all the arrangements on Roosevelt's behalf. These were orders coming to us from the very highest level, from the Prime Minister himself. I quickly realised the significance of that letter I had written to my mother the day before yesterday back in Dungallen House in Oban. This mission either succeeded or we died trying – there was no halfway house.

Harry Hopkins had first met Winston Churchill at 10, Downing Street earlier that year, on 10th January at the start of his first diplomatic mission to Britain which had lasted for five weeks. During that time the two men had become close friends and it was a friendship which was to prove a great asset to both their countries.
Hopkins returned to Britain in early July, just after

the German invasion of Russia. He had a number of issues to discuss with Churchill and was accompanied by several high ranking American military officers. At the top of his list of topics was Roosevelt's desire to meet with Churchill. At this time America was not at war and so such a meeting would need to be handled delicately and very discreetly if it was not to compromise the United States' already fragile neutrality. Hopkins was also instructed to discuss the American concern that the Near East campaign was absorbing a disproportionate amount of their war supplies.

Although not on his formal agenda, the situation in Europe following the German invasion was certainly on Hopkins' mind and, according to Churchill, "the first topic which he opened to me was the new situation created by Hitler's invasion of Russia". Hopkins was so concerned about this that he asked Churchill if it was possible to fly him [Hopkins] to meet Stalin and to return to Britain in a short space of time. Churchill told Hopkins that RAF Coastal Command flew PBY flying boats from Invergordon around the North Cape of Norway and could go on to Archangel on the White Sea.

However Churchill was not enthusiastic about the trip, which he saw as being a long and hazardous journey for his friend to undertake. Nevertheless Hopkins would not be put off and on the evening of 25th July, he and the new American Ambassador to Britain, John G. Winant, drafted a cable to President Roosevelt seeking authority for the trip. In part the cable read:

> *"I am wondering whether you would think it important and useful for me to go to Moscow. Air transportation good and can reach there in 24 hours......If Stalin could in any way be influenced at a critical time I think it would be worth doing by a direct communication from you through a personal envoy. I think the stakes are so great that it should be done. Stalin would then know in an unmistakeable way that we mean business on a long-term supply job. I, of course, have made no*

moves in regard of this and await your advice."

Within 24 hours Roosevelt had approved the mission, Churchill had made the arrangements and we were on our way. At the same time on that Sunday evening as we had been making the Catalina ready up at Oban, Churchill and Hopkins were walking on the lawn at Chequers, then as now, the Prime Minister's official country home. Churchill said to Hopkins, "Tell him, tell him that Britain has but one ambition today, but one desire – to crush Hitler. Tell him that he can depend on us. Goodbye and God bless you Harry."

Hopkins caught the train from London to Invergordon and the responsibility for getting him to Russia fell to us. Our American made PBY, known as the Catalina, was powered by two Pratt and Whitney radial, air-cooled engines which produced 175 mph at 7,000 feet for 2,350 miles which was just about enough to get us the 2,000 miles to Archangel. However with our full payload of fuel, supplies and extra passengers, we would only manage about 135 mph. It would take us about 20 hours to get to Archangel and at that speed we would be sitting ducks for the enemy fighter planes based in Norway. Our only real defence tactic would be to dive to sea level where, experience in the Mediterranean had shown McKinley that the much faster Italian and German fighters had been unable to pull out in time and as a result had crashed into the sea. It wasn't much but it was all we had because our guns were no match for the fighters.

In 1941, the German front line fighters were the Messerschmitt bf 109 which had a maximum speed of 375 mph and the Messerschmitt bf 110 with a maximum speed of 336 mph. The Me110 was a particularly dangerous enemy because it was armed with four machine guns and two 20mm cannon, most of which were forward facing. I was to tangle with a Me110 in 1944 when I had transferred back to Coastal Command from Bomber Command and was piloting a Lockheed Hudson on Air/Sea Rescue patrol looking for our pilots shot down over the North Sea the night before.

Catalina W8416 wallowed at her mooring off Invergordon in the evening light of Monday 28th July 1941. I looked out of a porthole to see a dinghy heading towards our boat and called to McKinley that our guests were arriving. As the dinghy drew alongside I guessed that the rather pale and ill looking man in the civilian suit and a trilby hat, was our V.I.P. Harry Hopkins, the personal envoy of The President of the United States of America. Mac McKinley took his arm and, helping him out of the pitching craft and across the watery gap, welcomed him to our boat. He was followed by a very smart officer in army uniform, his chest covered in medal ribbons, who rather struggled to get on board. This was General McHarney, Deputy to General George C. Marshall, the Head of the American Army. He was followed by another US Army officer, Colonel Paget, then attached to the Home Office and also displaying plenty of medal ribbons and finally Lieutenant Alison, a US Navy flyer. With all these people on board it was no wonder that Operations had selected us for 'just a skeleton crew'; any more weight and we wouldn't get off the water. The Top Brass were followed by a cascade of brief cases and suit cases which were thrown on board by the coxswain of the dinghy: the hatch was closed and we prepared for take-off.

I held the rank of Pilot Officer and as the Commissioned Officer not involved in the cockpit, I was the next most senior on board. It fell to me to ensure that our passengers were as comfortable as possible and had everything which they needed for the long flight. They settled themselves down for the journey and as I looked at them, the US President's right hand man, a three star General, a full Colonel and a Navy Lieutenant, the magnitude and importance of our mission fully dawned on me. I realised that this was not a social call on Stalin, but the sort of meeting upon which history is made and the war might depend: failure was not on the agenda. At the same time, I felt both honoured to have been chosen to be a part of it and intimidated by the magnitude of the responsibility which we all carried. After all, I was only 21 and McKinley was the oldest of us at 27.

At 20.30 hours, in the bright northern evening light, we taxied slowly from our mooring and a few moments later the Skipper opened up the engines. The Catalina gathered speed and the noise in the cabin increased as the sea rushed by underneath us, in an instant to be replaced by the comparative quiet of the engines as the flying boat lifted off the water. Then came an almighty bang which was heard throughout the boat; the nose anchor hatch had blown open allowing lengths of anchor chain to fall out and hammer on the windscreen. McKinley had no choice but to circle round, land, re-stow the chain and try again. This was not a good start to such a highly charged mission but happily the next take-off attempt was wholly uneventful and we were on our way.

An hour or so later Lt. Alison, looking rather alarmed, tapped the Skipper on the shoulder and said, "Hi, Cap'ain! Why are we only 500 feet above the water after so much flying time? We'll never get to Archangel unless we can do better than this." McKinley was completely relaxed about it and replied in his soft Irish accent, "If you mean we should go higher, I can assure you there are plenty of enemy patrols up there and they are definitely ready to see we do not get to Archangel". The US officer nodded and said, "Well I guess that makes sense. Thanks anyway", and left the cockpit.

We plotted a course which would keep us well away from the Norwegian coast. We flew in a broad northerly sweep between the Orkney and Shetland Islands, to the east of the Faeroes and then into the Arctic Circle and across the Norwegian Basin. We then turned east across the Lofoton Basin, passing within sight of Bear Island before turning south over the Barents Sea which would lead us into the White Sea and Archangel. The two Luftwaffe bases which we couldn't avoid were at Petsamo in Finland and at Kirkenes in Norway. We didn't have enough fuel to sweep over the Artic any further than we did: we would just have to take our chances against the fighters in the perpetual daylight of an Artic summer.

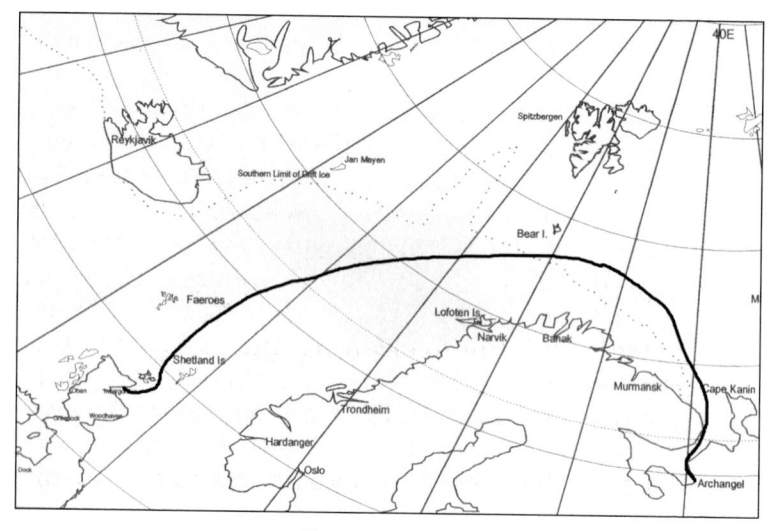

Route to Russia

As it transpired we had an entirely uneventful trip. We made extremely good time despite a patch of bad weather and with a tail wind to help us we continued to fly very low thus avoiding contact with the enemy and his radar installations.

Our American party though had not been warned about the extreme cold on these trips inside the Arctic Circle, even in July. I was wearing my Irvine flying jacket and trousers, a silk singlet and long johns, leather gloves and silk inners, my wool lined flying boots and helmet: the Americans were in their office uniforms and were shivering with the cold. I noticed that Harry Hopkins had a fair array of medication with him into which he had dipped a couple of times already: he didn't look a well man at all, especially not for a flight like this. I gathered together our sleeping bags and blankets and said to the Colonel that they might all like to climb into these and try to get some sleep on the bunks, particularly Mr Hopkins who was wearing only a thin lightweight civilian suit; after all he had left London on a lovely sunny July day. The Colonel took them from me saying, "That's awful kind of you, but what about you guys if we have all your kit?" I told him not to worry because I didn't think that any of us would be sleeping until we got to Archangel. He laughed and said, "Well that's kind of nice to know."

A few minutes later our Rigger brought them all some supper of hot soup and food from the thermos flasks we had loaded. Not long afterwards however, we rather unhappily ran into the awful weather with all the bumpy conditions which accompany bad weather in an aeroplane. It was too much for the Americans, except the Navy Lieutenant, and the Rigger's culinary efforts were wasted! I left Bill to clean up and encourage them all to lie down on the bunks and get some rest. Soon enough they were all catching up on lost sleep. We woke them up as we turned into the White Sea and set our course for the relatively short distance down the Russian coast to Archangel.

By now we were well inside Russian controlled air space and had climbed to 1,500 feet feeling safe from attack by German fighters. As we approached the White Sea we saw three Russian fighter planes in the distance, heading straight for us. Pilot Officer Owen fired the Verey pistol out of the starboard porthole, giving the recognition colours of the day. The seconds ticked by for what seemed an eternity; if these boys were not up to date, we were about to be blown out of the sky. Then, just as we began to conceive the worst, the pilot of the lead aircraft fired the same colours and they swept in beside us and escorted us in formation to Archangel. McKinley lined the big Catalina up for an excellent approach to touchdown on the water of the bay. Just as we skimmed along the blue sea the pilot of the front Russian fighter dived upon us from the stern with his undercarriage down. He was of course simply saying farewell, but he cut it a bit too fine and his wheel touched our mainplane causing slight indentations to it and ripping the aerial from its housing. McKinley was not put off and we taxied safely to the mooring, only too happy to have arrived after 20½ hours flying. It was 17.00 hours GMT.

The Russian High Command had turned out in force to meet us and a very noisy reception greeted our arrival.

Whilst the Russian military hosted Harry Hopkins and the American Officers, the crew were met on board our Catalina by the Mayor of Archangel and we were invited to a yacht which was tied up to the jetty close to our boat: this yacht, which was infinitely more comfortable than the flying boat, was to be our living quarters during our stay in Archangel. We were then all invited to a party given by an Admiral on his yacht which was also moored not far from the Catalina and, fortified by much vodka and cigarettes, he and his comrades were clearly determined to make the best of the opportunity which Hopkins' arrival had presented. We were allocated a stunningly attractive interpreter, who was assisted by several other equally attractive women, none of whom would have been any older than me. We were told that whatever we wanted, we were to ask our particular companion for and she would arrange it – no matter what it might be: of that we were left in no doubt! Hopkins however, despite his obvious exhaustion, was anxious to press on to Moscow as soon as possible but the interpreter told him that it was impossible to fly him to Moscow that night but that his flight was scheduled for 04.00 hours the next day. They weren't going to let him go that easily.

The reception celebrations had clearly started long before we had landed and after two hours a very senior Russian Admiral, armed to the teeth, collapsed on the floor suffering from nothing more than too much vodka. He was soon surrounded by more very good looking young women who were determined to revive him and engaged in a number of unusual First Aid procedures in their attempts to do so. I had always thought of Russian women as being very hard and all like the quintessential shot-putter. Not on this yacht they weren't; these girls were just as pretty and even more fun loving as any back home.

That night we were entertained to dinner by the Mayor and his senior Council Members. Like the reception on the yacht, the vodka flowed freely and it was very difficult to keep track of all that was happening. We were tired, hungry, had been to a party for two hours and the vodka was beginning to take its toll on our senses. This was our first introduction to real vodka and it was quite an experience. The meal was monumental with course after course. There was no wartime shortage here. Hopkins later observed of the meal: *"There was the inescapable cold fish, caviar and vodka. Vodka has authority. It is nothing for the amateur to trifle with."* How right he was. But for my own part I was just pleased to be there and enjoyed the endless food which was spread out in front of me. I thought that if my parents back in Shrewsbury, eeking out their weekly rations, could see me now they just would not believe it.

I sat next to my interpreter, a schoolmistress named Petrova, who was very friendly to me and talked a lot about life in Archangel. During the meal, a Russian uniformed officer came to our table and whispered something to the Mayor. Although I could not understand a word of Russian, it was clear from their whispered exchange that a matter of some importance was the subject of their conversation. I asked Petrova what it was all about and she said, "Just a moment, please." Although she smiled at me, there was no humour in her eyes. She then spoke to the Mayor briefly and with a composure which belied her years, she got to her feet and the room fell silent. "Gentlemen," she said, looking at McKinley, "we are deeply sorry about the accident with your aircraft this afternoon when you were coming in to land. This put all your lives at risk. The Russian High Command has just confirmed that the fighter pilot responsible will be shot." She sat down without any sign of emotion and everybody simply carried on talking as if she had merely announced the arrival of the next course. She turned to me and continued our conversation about the simple pleasures to be had from walking along the seashore.

I really could not comprehend that the pilot would be shot by his own side and I dismissed it all as offbeat Russian humour; and anyway I had drunk a lot of vodka, eaten a fabulous meal and was sharing the company of a very pretty and willing girl. Fifteen minutes later there was the unmistakeable sound of gunfire. My companion gently laid her hand upon my arm, "Excuse me;" standing up again she once more addressed the diners generally and McKinley in particular, "Gentlemen, the pilot has now been shot." The crew just couldn't believe what we had heard: had they really just shot the poor chap? Nobody in the room seemed to give a damn except us. Petrova, that part of her job done, returned to her primary role, that of cementing Russian-Anglo relations with me. I had another vodka and put the incident out of my mind for the night, no doubt helped by the insistent caress of her hand on my thigh beneath the tablecloth. Shortly afterwards the dinner party broke up and I saw that the rest of the crew were chaperoned as I was. For that's exactly what Petrova was: that was her job for the whole time I was at Archangel. The next morning I woke early, feeling again the tenderness of her lips on mine and the gentle caress of her fingers. The thumping in my head which the vodka had left slipped from my consciousness as I lay in her arms.

As I went about the various checks on the PBY that morning, I knew one thing was certain, the ruling classes in Archangel didn't share the austerity of the communist proletariat. Apart from the times when I was actually on board the Catalina, Petrova never left my side and since there was not much to do on the boat whilst Hopkins was in Moscow, we spent a lot of time together. We often walked out along the seashore she had talked about so much. Once, as we sat on the sand watching strange looking seabirds wheeling overhead, I asked her about her home and the war. A shadow momentarily flicked across her pretty eyes and she glanced passed me as she whispered, "Don't look round", with an urgency which took me by surprise. Her invitingly full red lips were trembling, almost imperceptibly, but I was so close to her that I could see the tiny movement. I wondered what I had said to frighten her so. A few minutes later we got up to wander back to the yacht. Then I saw the cause of her fear; an armed soldier whom I had not noticed before stood only a few feet away from us and could hear every word we said. He followed us back to the yacht as he had followed us along the shore. I was more careful for her after that as I began to realise what a dangerous job she was doing. My question to her was not in the script and I had put us both at risk.

Years later, when the Cold War had pitched East against West, I came to realise that everything which Petrova had said to me had been very heavily censored and intended to portray a very different picture than the reality of life in Archangel at that time. Her very presence with me was to ensure that I saw and did only what I was allowed to. Only in our whispered words as we shared my bed was she able to be herself. I have thought of her many times over the years and wondered what became of her. Did she survive the Nazis, the bombing, the hunger, the Communists and the Cold War? Only then did I realise why, as a token of her affection for me, she had secretly given me a beautiful seashell from the beach we had walked along on the day I left – she had nothing else of her own to give me.

Chapter 8

...... To The Kremlin

Hopkins and the American Officers, after only two hours sleep, were taken as planned at 04.00 hours to Archangel airport for the long flight to Moscow. There they were met by the American Ambassador, Lawrence A. Steinhardt and taken to the Embassy at Spasso House where the exhausted Hopkins was put to bed. Later that evening, a refreshed and now excited Hopkins left the Embassy with Steinhardt and a Russian interpreter for the Kremlin. It was not universally known then that Stalin, who was called Uncle Joe by the American public, was a ruthless tyrant responsible for the deaths of millions of his own people; but Hopkins knew more about him than most.

Stalin welcomed Hopkins to the Soviet Union and they immediately got down to the talks which Hopkins had gone all that way to have. He conveyed Roosevelt's diplomatic good wishes and informed Stalin that the President wished to urgently extend maximum aid to the Soviets. Hopkins asked Stalin what his immediate military needs were and the dictator, without hesitation replied, 20,000 anti-aircraft guns, heavy machine guns and a million rifles. This first meeting was fairly formal and lasted for about two hours.

The following evening, July 31st, Stalin and Hopkins met at the Kremlin alone apart from an interpreter. Stalin appeared to be more relaxed and gave Hopkins information on both the Russian and German divisional strengths, saying that Russia could mobilise more Divisions than Germany. He maintained that the Russian tanks were better than the enemy and he went on a long rigmarole about the strength of his Air Force, which Hopkins recognised as unrealistic but did not challenge him on it. Stalin dismissed outright German claims of the Soviets' air losses.

Stalin told Hopkins that the German claims of Russian

losses in combat aircraft were ridiculous and exaggerated, yet in June the Luftwaffe had bombed over sixty airfields and had destroyed nearly 2000 Soviet planes. During the next 24 hours another 1000 planes had been destroyed, mostly in the air. By the time Hopkins was in Moscow talking to Stalin, the Soviets had lost over 4,000 aircraft. Aviation historian, Von Hardesty maintained that, "For the Soviets, it was an air debacle of unprecedented scope and devastation". The Air Force Commander, Lieutenant General Kopets was so distraught he took his own life.

The Russian army made desperate attempts to break through the Panzer divisions which surrounded them, but this proved increasingly futile due to the lack of air cover. General Dmitry Pavlov, Commander of the Western Military District, was caught in a classic pincer movement by the German 2nd and 3rd Panzer Groups, commanded by Generals Guderian and Herman Hoth respectively. Pavlov managed to escape by moving his HQ to the city of Mogilev. He was there when Zhukov, the Chief of Staff called him from Moscow to ask if there was any truth in the German claim that he was surrounded by two armies east of Bialystok. Fatefully, Pavlov admitted that there was a large measure of truth in the claim. Together with several of his aides, Pavlov was ordered back to Moscow where Stalin had him shot.

When, back in Britain a few days later I learned of this, I knew that they really had shot the pilot who had collided with our Catalina. I felt sick; I thought it reeked of World War I buffoonery, but in the Cold War years ahead I came to realise that it was the butchery of dictatorship.

Stalin knew how desperate things were as he was talking to Hopkins, but he wanted to make a favourable impression on the man and clearly did. If he didn't succeed in doing so, he knew that the Americans would write off Russia and give all their support to Britain. At that time however, it was impossible for Hopkins to know that Stalin was telling him half-truths, misrepresentations and obvious omissions.

This last visit to the Kremlin had lasted about three hours and Hopkins left Stalin with a firm handshake. Stalin had been very confident about the war situation but had avoided being over confidant. Later Hopkins, in an American magazine, used this description of Stalin:

> "There was no waste of word, gesture, nor mannerism. It was like talking to a perfectly co-ordinated machine, an intelligent machine. Joseph Stalin knew what he wanted, knew what Russia wanted and assumed that you knew.........No man could forget the picture of the dictator of Russia as he stood watching me leave, an austere, rugged, determined figure in boots that shone like mirrors, stout, baggy trousers, and snug fitting blouse. He wore no ornament, military or civilian. He's built close to the ground like a football coach's dream of a tackle. He's about five feet six, about a hundred and ninety pounds. His hands are huge, as hard as his mind."

During his stay in Moscow, Hopkins had made the most of his opportunity and had called upon both the British Ambassador, Sir Stafford Cripps, later to become a member of Clement Atlee's post war Labour Government, and the Russian Foreign Minister, VM Molotov, better known for having created the 'Molotov Cocktail' during the Russian Revolution, a lethal concoction involving a glass bottle, some petrol, a rag and a match!

Whilst Hopkins had been in Moscow with Stalin, we had had our own problems and pleasures in Archangel. McKinley noticed that all was not right with the Catalina. He described it in his memoirs:

> "Later during refuelling I noticed the 'plane was very low in the water and after a check I found we had been given water instead of petrol. I quickly discovered from a pretty Russian interpreter that the Russian Authorities were determined to delay Hopkins' return to the UK. After a further one day delay and complete cleanout we were able to get airborne."

We were now unable to return to Britain as soon as we had planned and so were feted to another dinner. This had less of the formality of the previous occasion, since Hopkins had not yet arrived back from Moscow. It was the Catalina crew, our interpreters and as many from the Russian civil administration as could wangle their way in. As the vodka flowed again, the atmosphere became increasingly relaxed and we were invited to make impromptu speeches through our interpreters. Of necessity these were all very short and flattering to our hosts and our interpreters – after all, we did rather want to see our homes again. As one of the three British Officers present I knew that I would be required to say a few words; thus I had the great idea of introducing it with the customary "Ladies and Gentlemen", but in Russian. At an appropriate moment I asked Petrova to accompany me to the 'Gents'. She never batted an eyelid and obediently led the way. Standing in the quiet, rather draughty corridor outside the banqueting room, I asked her to pronounce what was written on each of the two doors. She told me, repeated it once and then did seem a little surprised when I simply thanked her and we returned to the dinner table. Whatever it was she thought I had in mind to do at that moment, returning to the table was clearly not one of them.

A few moments later I rose to my feet and very proudly began with the words Petrova had just recited to me. There was an icy quiet, agitation and some very red faces. With implacable calm, Petrova interpreted the rest of my drivel and we sat down to a stunned silence and hostile stares. It was very uncomfortable. "Why did you call them that at the beginning?" she whispered with desperate concern in her eyes. "What's wrong? We always start speeches with 'Ladies and Gentlemen'", I protested. As she looked at me her face relaxed and she started to giggle. She wrinkled her pretty retrousse nose and squeezed my arm, "Now I understand why we went to the corridor. I'll explain to them." She stood up and spoke rapidly in Russian for a few moments. As she sat down there was a great roar of laughter from the Mayor followed by much cheering and applause from around the room. "What's going on?" I asked Petrova. "I explained to them that far from insulting them, you had wished to show how much you appreciated their hospitality by greeting them as Ladies and Gentlemen in Russian and had visited the corridor doors to learn the words. You had not realised that on our lavatory doors we print 'Water Closets' for the Ladies and 'Urinals' for the Gentlemen! Now they think you are a truely worthy guest to have." Well done Petrova. She was still smiling about it long after we had returned to my cabin on the yacht for the night.

In the late afternoon on 1st August 1941 we left Archangel behind and took off into a gathering storm to retrace our flight through the Arctic Circle back to Scotland. On our return flight our payload was slightly different: Lieutenant Alison stayed in Moscow with the American Embassy staff and in his place we brought back a large quantity of very valuable platinum. Once more we managed to avoid all contact with the German Air Force but were nearly shot down by a Russian destroyer which failed to recognise our colour signals. We were along the Murman coast and still east of Kola Inlet. We dived down to sea level and although shrapnel had hit our mainplane, it caused very little damage. Nevertheless the firing did not cease until we had flown beyond the range of their guns. A careful lookout was maintained as the previous day aircraft from a British carrier had bombed airfields along the coast and we knew that the enemy would be out in force. Once more, we flew close to the surface of the sea to avoid radar and maintained radio silence.

Extract from Flight Lieutenant McKinley's log book 27th July to 2nd August 1941.

What a wonderful and welcome sight it was to see the shores of Scotland again. Showing our recognition colours whilst circling around Scapa Flow, we made a perfect landing in very rough and turbulent waters. Harry Hopkins, the 3-star General and the full Colonel all shook hands with McKinley, Pilot Officer Owen, myself and then with the rest of the crew. They thanked us for taking them to Archangel and for bringing them safely back to Britain – and they really meant it. It is difficult now to convey just how dangerous a mission this had really been. The fact that it had been uneventful didn't mean that it had been without danger. The route, the distance, the mission all meant that Churchill knew that this trip was too dangerous for his friend, but had mitigated it by giving him the best crew that Coastal Command could pick. We were careful and we were lucky, but we could so easily have be shot down at any time in more than 40 hours of flying over hostile waters. Even in July, the survival time in the waters of the Arctic Circle is only two minutes.

We had landed at Scapa Flow so that Hopkins could board the British Battleship HMS *King George V* for his return to America. The launch from KGV came alongside and I opened the hatch in the side of the Catalina. The launch was pitching badly in the choppy water and was unable to come in really close. Hopkins started to jump over the gap between the aircraft and the launch just as the launch and the flying boat moved apart in the swell. Conscious of the movement of the Catalina and seeing that he was about to fall head first into the waters of Scapa Flow, and despite my own tiredness, I jumped forward, put my arms around his waist and pulled him back into the body of the PBY. Unbeknown to me at the time, all this action was being filmed by a newsreel team in the Navy launch and years later the clip was shown on the BBC programme, 'Wings of War'. However, he ultimately made a hazardous leap over the open water between boat and aircraft and I remember thinking how utterly exhausted this man looked and what a huge strain he had undertaken for us all in this war. I knew that he had left his medicine in Moscow and that he was suffering badly, but had never complained to us once.

McKinley in his memoirs again, recorded the same impression:

> "My last glimpse of him showed him smiling and determined, though very dishevelled as the result of his wearying experience. As he waved us farewell we could not help feeling that very few persons could have taken what he had endured since we met at Invergordon on July 28th."

As soon as the launch bearing Hopkins and the others was clear of our boat we taxied round and took off for our base at Oban. By the time we landed at midnight we had all been awake for over 26 hours; all we wanted to do was to get to bed for a well-earned sleep, and sleep I did.

Harry Hopkins sent his report to Roosevelt and he had assured Stalin that the United States and Britain would do everything in the forthcoming weeks to send material to Russia. The Russian convoys started almost immediately and many in Coastal Command would be regular visitors to Archangel sooner than they might have wished.

Words are not enough to describe just how dangerous these convoys were. The waters of the Arctic are cold and dangerous at any time of the year, and the Germans were determined to harass these convoys every inch of the way: from the air, from the surface of the sea and from below the waves they attacked the Allied ships mercilessly and relentless. It was a living hell. The lads who sailed and escorted the convoys to Russia from Iceland and Loch Ewe, in the north west of Scotland were extremely brave. The conditions were atrocious and for most who ended up in the water, death was almost always inevitable, either from German machinegun fire or the cold. In the winter the water was so cold a man would die in it in literally seconds. We flew to Archangel in July more or less at sea level. Harry Hopkins and the American Service personnel with him were cold to their core and without our blankets and sleeping bags would have suffered hypothermia. How much worse it must have been when such conditions were experienced for days on end under constant attack from the enemy and the air was so cold that it would freeze a man's skin to the steel of the ship.

History has shown that the mission which we successfully fulfilled ultimately changed the course of World War II, but the sailors and airmen who delivered what we had started are the ones who deserve the recognition. Without their commitment during nearly four years of war in extreme hardship and danger, the Russians could not have resisted the Third Reich. There would have been no liberation of Europe. Those brave sailors and airmen should be properly recognised and honoured for their bravery.

David McKinley was later to achieve recognition when, in 1944 and now a Wing Commander, he piloted *Aries One*, a specially adapted Lancaster bomber, around the world and thus became the first RAF pilot to circumnavigate the globe. On 26th May 1945 he again flew *Aries One* 4,100 miles non-stop from The Yukon to RAF Station Shawbury in Shropshire, his home base, and in so doing became the first RAF pilot to fly over the Magnetic North Pole. Indeed much of the work he did on that trip forms the basis of long haul flight navigation today.

For my own part I did not return to Archangel. I doubt if I would ever have met Petrova again even if I had returned. We had both had a job to do: we had met, shared a tiny piece of our lives and then parted again. That was what war was like. At the time though I could never have guessed that by 2005 I would be the last surviving member of a mission which came to be recognised as playing such an important part in the outcome of World War II and thus the history of the world.

Press Report 1941

Russian medal 40th anniversary

Russian medal 50th anniversary

My Certificate and medals from the Russian government in recognition of my part in the Russian campaign

Chapter 9
Learning to Drive whilst Learning to Fly

Four days after our return to Oban the Adjutant told me that I had been recommended to train as a pilot. This was wonderful news; it was the very reason I had joined the RAF and was what I had wanted to do way back in 1939, which seemed an eternity ago now. The Adjutant then added that whilst I waited for my pilots' training course I would be posted to No.221 Wellington Squadron based at Limavady, Northern Ireland.

A week later I left Oban with much regret. I had really enjoyed my time with 210 Squadron and the posting had been very good to me. I had arrived as an LAC WOP/AG in January 1940 and 20 months later I was leaving as a Commissioned Officer. My friends gave me a great farewell party in the Mess the night before I finally left, although as the night wore on I came to remember less and less of it.

The next morning I walked down to the station at Oban for the last time and managed to get a seat in the front carriage of the train which was to be pulled by the little Caledonian Railway tank engine already noisily getting up steam. After a while the Station Master blew his whistle, the engine gave a short 'toot' and we set off for that lovely journey between the sea and the mountains, through Tyndrum Low Level station, Crianlarich and on to Glasgow Queen Street. This time I had to cross to Glasgow Central Station for my connection to Stranraer, and since the weather was fine and it was only a short distance between the two stations, I decided to walk.

Three quarters of an hour after I had walked onto the main concourse at Central Station we pulled away from the platform, crossed the River Clyde and swung away to Paisley and the west. The train took us through Lochwinnoch, which is now a RSPB Nature Reserve, then on to what was then the small town of Kilwinning, but which is now part of Irvine New Town, Britain's only coastal New Town. The track met the coast near Irvine just behind the ICI explosives factory, which if the Luftwaffe had bombed more successfully, would have simply left a hole in the ground where the town of Irvine had stood. I was sitting on the right hand side of the train and had a wonderful view of the Isle of Arran, the Sleeping Warrior, so called because it looks like a warrior lying on his back, asleep. We followed the seashore sometimes only feet away from the water, all the way down through Troon, Ayr and Girvan, where the line swung inland again and round to Stranraer, where I was to catch the ferry to Belfast.

From there I travelled to the village of Limavady, which is about 10 miles east of Londonderry, and arrived at the Officers' Mess. This was a very large mansion house in the country, set in its own grounds. There, over a beer, I met my new CO and many of the Squadron's pilots and navigators. The CO asked to see me in the morning and on my arrival at the aerodrome, which was some 2 miles away, I met the Adjutant. He explained to me that he was going into hospital for an operation and the CO wanted me to take over as Adjutant. This was not what I had in mind as I wanted to fly. I went to the CO, a Wing Commander and friendly type who called me Ted. For a Wing Commander to call a Pilot Officer by his Christian name was unusual outside the Mess, but that was his style. He explained his predicament that he needed an Adjutant and he needed me to do the job; I had no alternative but to accept. He then said, "Well done Ted. Look, I've left my papers in the Mess. Jump in my wagon and drive over to fetch them for me please."

I had never driven a car in my life but this was the moment I was to learn. I sat in the driving seat of the Winco's Hillman shooting brake looking to see where the ignition key went in. Having found the right place, I spotted a button which had 'starter' printed on it. I pressed it but all I got was a whining sound from a complaining starter motor. Then I saw the 'choke', pulled it out and pressed the starter button again. This time the engine fired into life, but I had no idea how to make it move.

What to do now? I was very conscious that if I wrecked the Winco's car, it wouldn't be 'Ted' that he would be calling me in a few minutes time. I thought back to the day two or three years ago I had sat behind my mother in her little Hillman Minx saloon car when she was being taught to drive and I desperately tried to remember some of the instructions which the driving instructor had given her. I put my left foot on the clutch, pressed it down to the floor and searched for first gear from the directions on the knob on top of the gear stick. My efforts were greeted with a terrible grating noise from an irritated gearbox. Oh God! I thought, I hope the Winco didn't hear that. I tried again and this time I got the hang of it; I pushed my right foot down gently onto the accelerator peddle but not far enough and the poor old Hillman set off in a series of jumps, like a kangaroo. We used to call it kangaroo petrol. I took my foot off the clutch and drove slowly around the perimeter track of the aerodrome - first on one side then the other. I drove around the track at least six times but in the end found that I could steer it reasonably well: I ventured out of the airfield and onto the main road, mounting the grass verge several times and narrowly missing the milkman with his horse and dray coming out of the gates to the Mess. I finally made it to the front door, ran in, picked up the CO's papers and got back into the Hillman before I forgot what I had learnt. I braved the main road again and, staying in second gear all the way, I finally and with a great sigh of relief, handed the CO his papers.

The Adjutant had already left and I had taken over his desk. The Station Warrant Officer knocked on the door of my office and walked in: he gave me the smartest salute I had ever seen. "Sah", he rapped, "I have an airman outside who has been placed on a charge. Will you deal with him, Sah?" I told him that I would – it was after all a rhetorical, not a multi-choice question. He explained to me that the airman had spent part of the previous evening in Port Stuart, drunk far too much and had been found by the Military Police, fast asleep on the pavement with vomit all over his uniform. I had not had to fulfil this role before and had no idea what an appropriate punishment would be, so I asked the Warrant Officer what he would do in such a case. He was visibly pleased that I had asked for his guidance and suggested that I confine the airman to barracks for 14 days. I thanked him, put on my peak cap and said, "Ok Warrant, show him in." In the passageway outside my office there was a barked command reminiscent of Corporal Simkiss, "*Atten-shun*! Airman, remove your hat. Quick march, left right, left right, left right. Halt!" A smart airman stood before me. He was clearly turned thirty years of age and here was I barely turned twenty-one. I told the airman to stand at ease. The Warrant Officer glanced at me because it was very unusual for a man on a charge to be stood at ease before the adjudicating Officer. He read out the airman's name, rank, number and the charge. I told the airman it was about time he grew up, got some sense of responsibility and remembered that there was a war on. "Yes Sir", he replied rather shamefacedly. "You will be confined to barracks for seven days." The Station Warrant Officer drew the airman to attention, "About turn", he shouted and marched him out of my office. As the door closed I heard the Warrant Officer say to the airman, "You're a lucky bugger. Our other Adjutant would have given you four weeks!" Well, maybe so, I thought to myself, but there but for the Grace of God go a lot of us in this war.

After I had been on the Station for a few weeks I began to get withdrawal symptoms; I needed to get back into the air. I wandered down to the Flights and went into the crew room where the various members of the crews gathered when on duty but not actually flying. George Ellis, a Flying Officer pilot was there as I hoped he would be. I told him that I had over 1,250 flying hours and was a qualified Gunnery Leader; would he mind if I joined his crew on his next flight? "Of course Ted, I would be delighted", he said, and three days later I was flying over the Atlantic in a Wimpy, the RAF's nickname for a Wellington bomber, for the very first time. I made five other such trips but after a year in Ireland I received a signal in my office to prepare the Squadron for a move to Reykjavik, in Iceland.

I was now a Flying Officer and the Winco made me CO Troopship for the voyage to Reykjavik, which apart from the authority it gave me, meant I had a lot more work to do. We left from Belfast in the Polish troop ship the *Sobieski,* and zigzagged to avoid the U-boats through the North Channel, up The Minches between the Inner and Outer Hebrides and then across the north Atlantic, this time passing to the west of the Faeroes and arrived in Reykjavik six days later. I am no sailor and was seasick for most of the voyage.

The Wimpys of the Squadron had already flown in to the airfield which was three miles outside Reykjavik. We were all billeted together in nissen huts, airmen and Officers alike. At night the temperature plummeted to well below freezing and even inside the corrugated iron huts it was bitterly cold. I didn't fly from here but was appointed to my old job, that of Adjutant.

Reykjavik, Iceland

It was early autumn 1942 and the cold was already a huge problem to us, especially at night, as the aircraft kept freezing up. Two days after our arrival one of our Wellingtons, fully loaded with fuel, ammunition and bombs took off for a night mission but it just could not gain any height. We ran out of the Flights and could hear the engines labouring as the pilot fought to get some lift. A few moments later there was a huge explosion and a ball of fire as the Wimpy hit the low hillside two miles from the airfield: another entire crew killed. The cause of the crash was icing on the leading edge of the wing.

The frozen sea off Iceland

As the Station Adjutant it was my duty to act as OC Funeral Party. At 22 years of age I had already seen too many of these, but we did what we had to do, said farewell to what was left of these friends and comrades and got on with the next job. There was little time or space for grief. War is like that.

Funeral Party for Wellington crew in Iceland

I had been in Iceland only a short time, when I received a signal ordering me to report to the Initial Training Wing, Torquay. At last I was on my way to be a pilot and back to school.

Fortunately, one of the Squadron Wellingtons was due back in the UK for a major service, so I was able to hitch a ride to RAF Grantham in Lincolnshire. From there I made my journey to Torquay by train. This was a long trip in wartime, with the inevitable delays caused by troops and equipment moving up and down the Country, as well as civilian passengers commuting to and from work each day. In due course the gleaming green, 'Castle' class steam engine slowed as we approached the outskirts of Torquay. It was autumn and the weather here was still lovely and certainly a lot warmer than it was in Iceland. As the valves opened and the white clouds of sweet smelling steam hissed from the engine, I opened the compartment door of the cream and chocolate coloured coach and stepped down onto the platform. The fronds of the palm trees barely moved in the gentle air of that late autumn afternoon and I could see why the GWR, on its advertising posters all through the 1930s had called this the English Riviera. It was straight out of an Agatha Christie novel.

I walked across to the Station Hotel and booked in; this was now the Officers' Mess. I dropped my kit in my room and went down to the bar where others on the course were gathering for an evening drink; we were a mixed collection of Army, Navy and RAF Officers. I met up with Squadron Leader Peter Gee, a permanent commissioned Officer and an accountant in the Service; he was a near neighbour of my parents in Shrewsbury. He must have been very keen to fly because after qualifying he was going to be demoted to Pilot Officer.

I became friendly with Peter Cranley, also a Flying Officer WOP/AG and ex RAF Cranwell boy apprentice. He had seen service on Blenheim 1V light bombers and we remained pals throughout our Pilots' course. Sadly he crashed in the Near East in 1944 whilst flying a group of senior Officers to a conference. Everyone on board the DC3 Dakota transport plane was killed including Peter.

Peter Cranley (right) and self

There was none of the modern idea of 'bonding' sessions or team building exercises on this course; next morning we were straight into the classroom and sitting a maths exam. Happily we all passed. For the next five weeks we were classroom based and studied hard. At the end of that phase of the course we were posted to Canada to learn how to fly.

We set sail from Liverpool aboard one of the most famous and luxurious ocean going liners of the day, the RMS *Queen Mary*. She was the last pre-war holder of the Blue Riband, taking it from the French liner *Normandie* in August 1938. At least it would have been a luxurious trip had she not been converted to a troop ship in the summer of 1940. By the end of the war she had sailed over 600,000 miles and carried nearly 800,000 troops.

As we left the Mersey we began our zigzag course across the Atlantic. The *Queen Mary* was only lightly armed and we had no escort. It was considered unnecessary because she was simply too fast for escorts and U-boats alike. She had a service speed of 29 knots and was easily capable of over 30 knots; she was after all, the Blue Riband holder. We berthed at St. John's in Newfoundland five days later. We then travelled by train to a Transit Camp at Monkton, in Nova Scotia and being junior Officers we were placed in the Junior Officers' Mess.

The airmen who had qualified as pilot/navigators and who had received their Commission on passing out, were still dressed in their airmen's uniform. These Officers were also billeted in this Mess but to distinguish them as Officers, they wore a white band around their caps; there must have been at least 100 to 150 of them. However Peter Cranley, who had been an Officer for sometime was rather put out by this and asked to see the Group Captain. He complained that it was simply not good enough that we were mixed up with them in this way. We had both done a tour of operational flying and we should be treated accordingly. He told the Group Captain that, in his view, it was nothing short of a disgrace. Fortunately for Cranley the GC saw his point of view and arranged for the Adjutant to issue us with dollars and railway vouchers and sent us off to tour Canada for three weeks.

We travelled 1st class in a Pullman coach from Monkton to Montreal. About two hours from the big city, as we waited to be seated in the Dining Car we found ourselves standing next to two very attractive Canadian girls. Never one to let a chance go by, I said cheekily, "You want to give this country back to the Red Indians." This was in the relaxed days before political correctness, when people could talk to strangers without fear of being rebuked. The girls both laughed and we joined them at their table for dinner. We passed a very enjoyable two hours in their company during which time they told us a lot about Canada. We arrived in Montreal at 20.30 hours, said our farewells to the ladies and booked into a hotel for the night. We were here to enjoy ourselves and after a wash and brush up we went into the city to join the nightlife.

The next night we caught the Canadian Pacific train west with the intention of travelling to Banff for Christmas, which was in ten days time, but by one of those great coincidences of real life, who should also be on the train but the two girls we had met the previous evening. Betty Griffiths and her friend Peggy were great company and in the luxury of the public areas and the comfort of our compartments, we shared and enjoyed their company for four days as we journeyed across Canada.

The train had those wonderful viewing coaches and the girls often took us into one or another of them to point out the magnificent scenery and landmarks as the countryside unfolded before our eyes. One of my great lasting memories of the journey is simply the scale of the Canadian prairies: they stretched as far as the eye could see. No wonder the North American Indians had fought so long and hard to retain their hold on this land; who wouldn't? When we got to Moose Jaw, about half way between Winnipeg and Calgary, Betty handed me a telegram from her parents. It read simply, "*Yes, certainly bring RAF boy home for Christmas.*" I was delighted. Not long after this, Peggy had a similar telegram from her parents inviting Peter for Christmas too. Well, that was us both fixed up for Christmas and things just kept on getting better.

Betty and I travelled to the end of the line on the west coast at Vancouver. There we caught the ferry to Victoria on Vancouver Island. As we walked down the gangway I saw a very large and highly polished car, not unlike a Rolls-Royce, strategically parked in front of us at the bottom of the gangway with an equally smartly turned out chauffer, clearly waiting for an important passenger from the ferry. Betty half turned towards me and with her infectious laugh and twinkling eyes said, "Oh good, daddy's sent the car for us." Of course I thought she was joking, but sure enough her father's chauffer was waiting for us. It reminded me of scenes from the Pathe or Movietone newsreels at the cinema when the 'stars' came off the great ocean going liners in New York or Southampton. We were whisked away and in no time at all had left the town behind and were driving through more beautiful countryside. Betty held my hand and we just sank into the moulded leather upholstery of the back seat and once again I thought about the disbelief of my mum and dad in Shrewsbury. Fairly soon though the car slowed and turned through an imposing gateway and up a long driveway to Betty's mansion house home, where I was most warmly welcomed by her mother and father.

This was Christmas 1942 and, following the Japanese attack on Pearl Harbour in Hawaii a year earlier on 7th December 1941, America had entered the war. In many ways it was a great relief to us because since the fall of France in May 1940, the British Empire had stood alone against the might of the German, Italian and Japanese war machines. Certainly Betty's father had no doubt that, just as in World War I, once the United States were involved victory was a matter of when, not if.

Betty's father with his favourite dog showing his mansion in the background

Betty's father had been born in London's East End in the early 1890s. He had served in the army during World War I on the Western Front, but after the war had found it difficult to get a job in 'the land fit for heroes'. For a time he was a barrow boy selling fruit on the streets of London before emigrating to Australia where he became involved in fruit growing. He bought some land, put a manager in charge and moved to Canada where he built a canning factory to can the fruit he was growing in Australia. He was a businessman who, from small beginnings, now employed a large number of staff including a chauffer and had built the mansion house on Vancouver Island where they lived. Betty was his only daughter and was married to a doctor who had volunteered for war service, held the rank of Major in the Canadian Army Medical Corps and was serving in France.

On Christmas morning I came down to breakfast at about 9.30 and there, on the table in front of where I was to sit, wrapped up in glittering paper complete with labels saying, "Ted. Merry Christmas", were so many presents it was overwhelming: a Remington electric razor, a shirt, slippers, various toiletry items and so on. I could hardly believe I had met such kind people. Later that day Betty's parents went over to visit some friends on the far side of Vancouver Island, saying that they were sure we would be glad of some time together alone. As we waved them goodbye, standing on the steps of the mansion house, I remember thinking how strange her father looked behind the wheel of the big limousine: it was Christmas Day and the chauffeur was at home with his family.

Betty and I loved and laughed and partied over Christmas and the New Year but finally had to say goodbye when I received a telegram to report to Dewinton, a small airfield 5 miles from Calgary, my Elementary Flying Training School. I had had a simply wonderful time with Betty that Christmas and she even took me to see *Casablanca,* starring Ingrid Bergman and Humphrey Bogart. Her parents had opened their home to me and treated me with a kindness I have never forgotten. A long way from home and in a strange country, it could have been a very lonely Christmas for me, but instead it was a memorably happy one. On one occasion Betty's father dressed up in my uniform and I in her mother's clothes just so that we could have a photograph of the scene. I still have that picture. Betty took me round her friends and for a few days I lived and played in the world of the fabulously wealthy; but everyone was so pleasant and natural about it all; I was never made to feel anything but welcome. We enjoyed each other's company and all the seasonal parties which just seemed to run into each other but sadly it all came to an end and I had to go back to work and back to war. I did see Betty once more after that holiday. Before I returned to England at the end of my pilots' course, she travelled all the way from Vancouver Island to Monkton on the Atlantic coast, to spend my last two days and nights in Canada with me...

In Flying School we were taught the fundamental principles of flight, played around on the Morse Code keyboard but most importantly we got to fly and we started in Tiger Moths. In an open cockpit wearing my

Irvine jacket, goggles and helmet, and feeling for all the world like Biggles, I was taught to fly. My instructor was a Flying Officer who sat in the front seat of the plane and, looking mainly at the back of his head and the instruments in front of me, I learnt the procedure for taxiing.

After a practice or two at that we took off and at 3,000 feet and away from the airfield he asked me to take the joystick with my first finger and thumb so that I could get the feel of the aircraft. Once I had the feel of it I heard his voice through the earphones of my helmet say, "I have it", and he showed me how you kept the aircraft straight and level followed by gentle one rate turns to the left and then to the right. Then it was my turn again and I took over and tried to master what he had done, in time quite successfully.

The next hour of instruction taught me how to take-off and land. Apart from the vital instructions prior to take-off, I was taught how to line the aircraft up by picking out a point ahead for guidance, open the throttle to maximum revs and as the aircraft moved forward, control its direction with the rudders. Then as the speed built up, with finger and thumb, gently push the joystick slightly forward allowing the speed to increase and then gently moving the stick backwards slightly. The plane eased off the ground and was airborne. The 'circuit and bumps', as it was called, was practised until near perfect 3-point landings could be achieved.

Before I was allowed to go solo, instructions were given in steep turns, glide approach, stalls and spins, that is, how to get out of a stall and spin position. After six hours with my instructor, I landed and taxied to the position for take-off again. Then to my great surprise and excitement he slipped out of his harness and said through the intercom, "Now you have a go yourself." With that he jumped down from the little Tiger Moth and I was all alone, ready to make my first solo flight. The sweat poured from my forehead underneath the helmet as I thought about the procedure I had practiced so often. It all came together well and I made a perfect take-off. I climbed straight up to 600 feet and with a gentle turn to the left and still climbing I levelled out on my crosswind leg at 1000 feet. Beyond the boundary of the airfield I completed a gentle turn to the left to line up on the downwind leg and parallel with my landing line. Then, past the boundary at the other end of the airfield I carried out another gentle turn to the left, throttled back slightly to loose height and remained on this heading, still slowly loosing height until I was nearly level with my position to make my landing approach. I carried out another gentle turn to the left and finally was straight on my approach path. I put down my flaps, throttled back and made a gentle powered approach. As I came up over the boundary fence I shut down the throttle and glided in, checking back gently on my stick at stalling speed I brought the stick towards me and made an absolutely perfect 3-point landing. Taxiing round I picked up my instructor who was delighted with my performance: he took the aircraft back to the Flights and we had a well-earned cup of tea.

Dual and solo flying continued for 5 weeks learning cross-country flights, map reading, aerobatics including inverted flying, loops, spins, rolls, stalls, the lot. My other flying was in a static machine on the ground called a 'Link Trainer'. This was an early flight simulator where all the flying was by instruments. At the end of the course I passed out with above average marks; I was very definitely pleased with my examination results. I was posted to an airfield at Moose Jaw to learn to fly twin-engine aircraft, an Airspeed Oxford.

The basic training procedure was very similar, but the aircraft was very different. There was no joystick but a wheel instead; the pupil sat on the port side of the cockpit and the instructor, with similar controls, sat on the starboard side instead of one behind the other as in the Tiger Moth. In a twin-engine aircraft take-off was achieved by slowly opening the two throttles evenly together and gently easing back on the wheel. I went solo after 5 hours of dual instruction. As before, steep turns, stalls, corkscrews and so on were taught and navigational cross-country flying was a must, including flying by the compass. Very quickly over 60 hours of dual and solo flying was notched up, as too were many hours of instrument flying under covers to prepare us for night flying. Dual instruction at night was a stunning introduction to a whole new world of flying and I will never forget my first solo night flight. Little did I know it then but the night flying skills I learnt at Moose Jaw would twice save my life and lead me to meet the girl I would one day marry.

Four half days each week were spent in school learning the principles of flight, navigation, both by dead reckoning and the stars, meteorology, the mechanics of the engine and so on. At the end of the course there was a written examination; the minimum pass mark was 65%. Then it was on to the Chief Flying Instructor practical examination; take-off and landing, steep turns, stalls, single engine flying, precautionary landings, map reading, navigational cross-country flight, night flight and the like were all were included. Once again it was the CFI skills I learned here which would save my own life and the lives of my crew one day in the not too distant future.

At the end of the course those of us who had passed had a full 'Passing Out' parade, complete with military band. An Air Commodore presented us with our Wings and we were all jolly proud of ourselves; it had been a very intensive course. I felt enormous pride as I removed my Aircrew half wing and instead stitched onto the left side of my tunic above the breast pocket, my hard earned double wings.

In due course we arrived back at Monkton and this time Cranley wangled us to stay in the Senior Officers' Mess for our two days there. At least he stayed there; I spent my time with Betty. After that we were on the train to St. John again to catch the *Queen Mary* for the trip back across the Atlantic to the UK and home. We were granted 14 days leave; it was 11th June 1943, I was promoted to

Flight Lieutenant with two thick blue rings on my sleeve and I was going home to my parents' house.

Although it was overcast when I arrived at Shrewsbury railway station I decided to walk across town. I hadn't told my parents that I was coming home in case anything had happened crossing the Atlantic: there were still plenty of U-boats about, even though they had taken a real pounding during the first week of May off Newfoundland, when 6 were sunk, another 17 were damaged, some severely and two were rammed. It was to prove to be all too much for Admiral Donitz's wolf packs and they gave up on the North Atlantic convoy routes, although we didn't know that at the time.

I walked through the back door and into the kitchen, dropping my case onto the tiled floor as I had done with my football kit 10 years earlier. I could hear my mother talking in the next room as my father helped her to set the table for their evening meal. I leaned against the doorpost of the dining room, with my Officer's cap pushed back on my head and said, "You're a place setting short, mum." I can still see my mother's face light up as she came across the room to greet me. My father noticed the Flight Lieutenant's rings on my sleeve and the pilot's wings on my chest and proudly, but with a reserve which my mother had discarded, shook my hand and congratulated me. By then my mother had composed herself somewhat, "You might be a pilot Edward, but you will still take your cap off in my house." Oh well, she was still my mum and I was still her youngest son. She was understandably always overjoyed whenever any of her children came home on leave and I know that we were a lucky family because all four of us survived the war.

My next posting was to RAF Condover, near Shrewsbury and so only about five miles from where my parents lived. Still flying Airspeed Oxfords, I was now on the Advanced Flying Course where we learnt the finer rudiments of piloting an aeroplane, with particular emphasis on cross-country and night flying navigation.

It may seem strange now that so much time was given to training pilots in these two skills, but in order to understand why, three things must be remembered. Firstly, at that time combat aircraft had very few instruments and certainly none of the modern sophisticated navigational equipment. Most of our navigation was done with map, compass, protractors, visual observation, mathematics and, it has to be said, a fair amount of luck. Secondly, we were at war and there was a blackout in operation. When we flew over the countryside it was pitch black below us; there were no streetlights to give us a clue as to where we were; it just looked like flying over a sea of ink. Thirdly, the enemy was just as careful at concealing his towns and cities and so good navigation and night flying skills were essential to a successful bombing raid and to offer any hope of a safe return home. Finding the target was only half of the task, finding home in the dark afterwards was just as difficult and the navigator may have been killed or injured.

For the next part of the course I was posted to the other side of Shrewsbury, to RAF Shawbury, which today is the multi-service helicopter training base with Army, Navy and Air Force pilots being trained there. This was the Beam Approach Course and entailed listening through the earphones of the headset to *'dit dah'* *'dit dah'* and *'dah dit'* *'dah dit'* followed by *'dah-dah-dah'*, a humming sound and *'dit-dit-dit-dit'*. These sounds would indicate to the pilot that he was flying on the beam and would be able to approach the runway 'blind' down to about 50 feet. 'Health and Safety at work', 'Risk Assessment' and 'taking reasonable care' were not phrases in our vocabulary, if they had been we would never have taken off in the first place. All good fun really!

60 years later in 2003, I was to sit in the Senior Officers' Mess at RAF Shawbury and have lunch with the Commanding Officer, Group Captain Mark Wordley. By then I was Chairman of 210 [FB] Squadron Association and I presented a limited edition framed print of a Catalina to the Station. Around the table with us

that day were my solicitor friend Ken Ballantyne, a Squadron Leader, a Flight Lieutenant, a Navy Lieutenant Commander and an Army Major. As we talked about operational flying, the development of the RAF and the new multi-Service helicopter role, one thing became abundantly clear: the technology had moved on from 1943 out of all recognition, but the basic job of the pilot and the mission remained the same.

I was then posted to the Operational Training Unit, or OTU as it was known. We were now at the top of our flying curriculum and I was introduced to my crew, who turned out to be a grand team of chaps. It was now that I at last got behind the controls of a Wellington bomber, that wonderful design of Barnes Wallis: lamentably, he was not Knighted until long after the war. Barnes Wallis is fondly remembered by the pilots of Bomber Command for his design of the geodetic, or cross lattice, construction of the hull and wings of aircraft, most notably the Wellington. This design gave great strength, but was very light and so made the aeroplane both manoeuvrable and strong. There were many crews who limped home in a battered and shot up Wellington bomber which, but for Barnes Wallis' design, would never have made it back across the English Channel or the North Sea. In a few weeks time we would be one of those crews.

Sir Barnes Wallis is of course best remembered by the public for designing the bouncing bomb used by the Lancaster bombers of No.617 Squadron in the Dam Busters' raid on the Mohne, Eder and Sorpe dams of the Ruhr valley on the night of the 16th May 1943 where Squadron Leader Guy Gibson won his VC. Gibson failed to return from a mission the following year and was presumed killed in action. The raid did affect the German war effort, but had an even bigger propaganda impact. It cost the lives of eight Lancaster crews, including that of 'Dinghy' Young, the rowing Blue who got his nickname from having ditched his aircraft in the sea more often than anyone else. Once more his Lancaster was so badly damaged that he had to ditch in the North Sea on his homeward journey but sadly this time neither he nor his crew survived. The raid also took the lives of several hundred German civilians and part of the prisoner workforce who were billeted nearby and yet even to this day there is no memorial to the raid at the Mohne Dam.

After a few more weeks of navigation and bombing practice we were all posted out to our Bomber Command Operational Stations.

Top: The Mohne Dam on the 17th May 1943 the morning after No.617 Squadron's visit; bottom: On the 11th November 1956 showing the rebuilt centre section and the depth to which the water had risen (photo: John Ballantyne)

Chapter 10

Bomber Command and Air/Sea Rescue

RAF Wellington bomber

As I sat high off the ground at the controls of my Wellington bomber, I casually looked to my left at the port wing and for a few minutes watched the propeller blades gently spinning as the Vickers engine idled. I had flown as second pilot to the Flight Commander on three trips before I was skipper of my own plane with my own crew. My crew were a good bunch; we had been together for several weeks now and so far we had had a pretty steady run of missions. Through my headset I could hear them talking to each other as they and my second pilot prepared for take off. Despite our target that night, they were in good spirits. Our trips had been straightforward enough, take off, find the target, drop the bombs and go home. We had been shot at each night by the German ground defences but the flak had generally not been too bad and we had been lucky.

Bombing Up - loading a Wellington with 2,000lbs of bombs

Tonight would be different though; tonight we were going to bomb the Krupps' factory at Essen in the heart of the Ruhr. I thought back to the afternoon's briefing session and all the information which the Operations' Officer had given to us when he announced the target. The details of the defence ack ack and searchlight installations, fighter strengths, weather conditions and so on. Although there would be bands of cloud, it would be clear over the target and there would be a full moon. "Is there any good news, Sir?" The Hon. Stanley Malpass, Bt., had asked in his beautifully rounded Etonian accent. We had all laughed and it eased the tension; he had said what we were all thinking. Like many RAF Squadrons, we had our share of the aristocracy on active service.

It hadn't taken the Germans many weeks to rebuild the stricken factory output after No.617 Squadron's visit to the Mohne and Eder dams in May, and now we were hitting those factories again every night we could. During 1943 the Americans had been carrying out precision daylight raids with their B-17 Flying Fortresses and B-24 Liberators but raids into Germany beyond the range of fighter protection were proving too costly in lives and aircraft. Consequently the Americans pulled back and concentrated on targets which they could reach with fighter escort. That meant that our own night time raids were stepped up to keep the pressure on the German war material production factories of the Ruhr. However this was to be one of the last missions to be flown by Wellingtons into the German heartland because the larger and heavier Lancaster and Halifax bombers had taken over that role.

The policy of Bomber Command and the USAAF at that time was quite simply one of round the clock bombing to weaken the German war output and morale. After the war, and particularly after the raid on Dresden in east Germany, which started at 9pm on 13th February 1945 when 786 RAF bombers dropped 2690 tonnes of bombs from low level [there was no Luftwaffe or ground defences by then] in which somewhere between 25,000 and 200,000 people died, this policy was seriously questioned. But at the time it was considered the right way to do things and for years it had been Britain's only way of carrying the war to Germany.

Loading a Wellington with the Big One

I was snapped out of my reverie by a disembodied voice in my headset using our call sign. It was the WAAF in the control tower; we were cleared for take-off and I signalled to the ground crew for chocks away. I eased the levers forward and gently opened both throttles; the heavily laden Wellington, carrying 2 tonnes of bombs plus ammunition for the front and rear guns and fuel to get us to Essen and back, began to move. We took our place in the line of Wimpys waiting to take off and a few moments later we were careering down the runway. As the tail wheel came up off the ground she gave a little wiggle. I let her build up speed and felt her lift off the runway; we were up. My co-pilot raised the undercarriage as we climbed to take our place in the formation of aircraft droning across the blanket of pitch darkness below us that was East Anglia.

On our way - Wellingtons leaving on a bombing raid

After a time we crossed the coast and that part of the North Sea where it begins to narrow towards the Straights of Dover, in what is better known as sea area Thames in the shipping forecast, glinted in the rising moonlight and stretched out before us like a piece of frosted glass. We had been joined by Lancasters and Halifaxs and were making for the mouth of the Rhine to lead us into

Germany's manufacturing heart, the Ruhr Pocket. We knew that once we crossed the coast of occupied Europe on this route we would meet the enemy. Our cruising height was about 14,000 feet and we stayed well above the early flak which was put up along the way by the ground defences.

In April 1943, just before the Dambusters' raid, Wing Commander Leonard Cheshire [later to be Sir Leonard Cheshire] had taken command of No.617 Squadron. Flying the very fast Mosquito, he pioneered new marking methods which drew us much more accurately onto the targets. In short, the pathfinder Mosquitoes went ahead of us to the target and marked it with flares and incendiary bombs. By the time we got there the whole place was lit up like a Christmas tree. Cheshire left No.617 Squadron in July 1944 with a VC, a DFC and two bars to his DSO. After the war he and his wife Sue Ryder devoted themselves to charity work. He was subsequently Knighted for this work and Sue Ryder charity shops are a familiar sight in many High Streets today.

As we got near to the Ruhr, the formation of aircraft divided with some of the bigger bombers going on further into the Ruhr to other targets. We turned away from the Rhine towards Essen and began to descend to a bombing height. The flak here was everything we had been expecting and worse. By now it was bursting all around us and I was having some difficulty holding the plane steady for the bomb aimer to do his job. I looked around me at the other aircraft close by. I could see them clearly in the light from the fires on the ground and the bursts of flak. One of our Wellingtons was just overhead with his bomb doors open; we were far too close for comfort. I eased the Wimpy out of his drop line just in time to see a blinding flash in the sky above us. Bits of burning aircraft came raining down all around us: two of our bombers had collided and with fuel, bombs and ammunition had simply exploded. This was always a risk in massed bombing raids especially at night and cost many lads their lives. "Hold her steady, Ted," came the voice of Bill Evans, our Welsh navigator and bomb aimer, in my headset, "more flak coming up. Hell, that was near". Suddenly the whole cockpit was awash with light; we were in the full beam of the searchlights. This wasn't just the overspill from the beam but the full glare of the light. I knew the deadly 20mm ack ack guns on the ground would turn on us and almost at once the flak increased even more. I couldn't start to weave because we were making our run; my job was to hold the Wellington straight and steady so that we could drop our bombs on the first run and get out of there. We didn't want to have to go round again. I just hoped that we could drop our bombs before the gunners on the ground got our range.

"Bomb doors open. Keep her like that." Even as Bill's words were sounding in my ears the Wellington gave a great lurch and my co-pilot said, "Watch out we've been hit, Ted. Starboard engine." The dials in front of me told me what he was seeing, that the engine was still working but we were losing power from it. The noise was deafening. All around us there were shells bursting in loud explosions, the roar of the engines, normally balanced, were now out of kilter and the wind was whistling through the open bomb doors.

"Ok everybody, its not serious. We're still on target run. Carry on Bill, but hurry if you can," I said. "Steady, steady, hold her......bombs gone!" The words we were all waiting to hear from Bill came through the intercom as the Wellington bucked with the release of 2 tonnes of high explosive from her racking.

The flak was now very heavy and concentrated as we were still fixed by the beam of several searchlights. There was another explosion just beneath us and the aircraft shook again; the bomb doors mechanism was damaged and they wouldn't close. No matter what I did, I couldn't get them shut. The emergency gear had failed too. We were now in trouble because the doors were slowing us down significantly and even if we escaped the flak we would be a sitting duck for a night fighter. It was like dragging a parachute behind us.

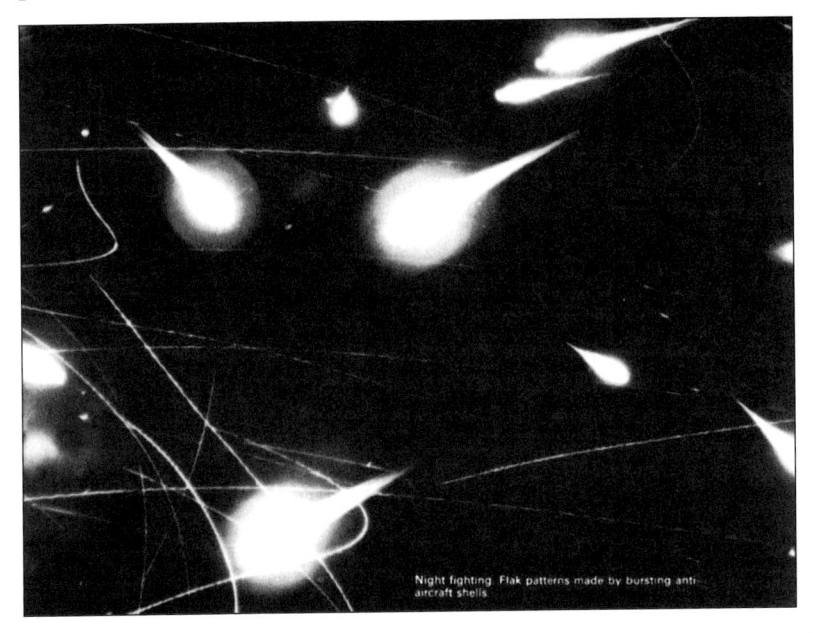

Night fighting. Flak patterns made by bursting anti-aircraft shells.

ACK! ACK!

I banked the Wimpy round and away from the ack ack and set the course for home. This had to be a different course from the outward leg, otherwise returning aircraft would run into later waves of bombers approaching the target. By now we were so slow that we were more or less on our own. Occasionally we would see another aircraft pass by in the distance, but essentially we would have to take care of ourselves. For a time all went well, although the strain of holding the bomber straight, with one engine giving less power than the other was beginning to tell on my arms and legs. It was also bitterly cold at this height in winter with the bomb doors open. We were now flying above one of those flat bands of cloud which the Met Officer had told us to expect. I looked out across the spectral scene beneath us, shining like a silver tablecloth in the brilliant moonlight. As I reflected upon the beauty and tranquillity of our surroundings my stomach turned over and I gave an involuntary shiver. I had suddenly realised how we would look from outside the aircraft and from some way off: we were the unmistakeable silhouette of a lone British Wellington bomber picked out in black against that silver tablecloth and at the mercy of every German night fighter within fifty miles. We needed to loose height, but we also needed to know where we were. The oil pressure was dropping in the starboard engine too, which was a worry but at least there was some power from it. I didn't fancy trying to fly all the way back home on one engine. "Skipper, the clouds are breaking up and we should be able to see the coast in about 10 minutes." Bill Evans, back at his navigator's table from the bomb aimer's bubble was guiding us back home on a course which avoided built up areas as much as possible, but we weren't quite sure exactly where we would reach the sea. Ideally we would like to have swung out to the north of Amsterdam, but the Wimpy was too badly damaged for that, so we were aiming for north of Ostend.

Just as I was beginning to think that we might make it home all right, John Arbutt, my rear gunner shouted, "Fighter closing in on the starboard beam. It's a 110, coming in fast, now! Swing her to starboard Skipper." The problem we had here was that Wellingtons had no guns pointing sideways, they were at the front and the rear and the Luftwaffe pilots knew this and so tended to attack from the side if they could.

Well this pilot should really have plucked us out of the sky that night, but either he was not very experienced or, more likely, had hadn't calculated that we were flying as slowly as we were. Either way, his burst of cannon fire missed and he overshot us without our firing in reply. Perhaps the German thought our guns were out of action because he banked round and came straight at us from the rear this time. I was getting a running commentary in my headset from John as he opened fire on the Messerschmitt, then I felt the plane stutter and heard a low groan.

"John, John. Are you hurt?" "It's my legs, Skip, and the guns. They won't move". The Me flew directly over us to bring his rear gunner into range, but as he flashed passed a few feet over my head, our front gunner was quicker and opened fire first. He hit the Me dead centre underneath and it twisted away. But we had got our own problems now; as well as wounding John and disabling the rear guns, the 110 pilot had also fired cannon shells into our main cabin and we were on fire with flames licking at the walls and roof. I could feel the heat behind me. I saw the fighter going down with a trail of fire behind it. I have no idea whether the pilot and crewman got out and didn't care; I was concerned only for my own crew. "Good shooting. Anyone else hurt back there?" I did a roll call and thankfully there were no further casualties. The flight engineer and navigator were dealing with the fire in the middle of the plane and I sent my co-pilot, Tom 'Sandy' Sands back to see how badly injured John Arbutt was.

Sandy opened the turret door and eased John out from his seat behind the guns. He had shrapnel in both legs and right arm. He was losing blood and baling out was not an option for him. Sandy patched him up as best he could and with the help of the other two, who had by now managed to put the fire out, made John more comfortable. A few minutes later I saw the pale string of waves breaking on a shoreline far below us. We needed to make more progress than we were up here and so I decided to go down to sea level where the wind resistance on the open bomb doors would be a lot less. It would also reduce some of the burden on the starboard engine.

I eased the Wellington down until we were almost wave hopping, but I knew that the sea was calm and I also knew from my days in Coastal Command that we were less of a target for fighters at this level. It wasn't too long before we sighted land and Bill got a fix on our exact position. We made straight for the nearest airfield and radioed our plight to the control tower. We landed safely much to everyone's relief and were quickly surrounded by ambulances and fire tenders.

John was whisked away to a nearby hospital and that was the end of his flying days. Although he recovered, they could not safely remove all the shrapnel from one of his legs and for the rest of his life he walked with a limp. He was 23 and before joining the RAF had played rugby for his hometown of Clitheroe in Lancashire. Next morning, after our debrief and before joining the rest of my crew in the 15cwt truck that would take us back to our own base, I went and had a look at the old Wellington, G for George as she stood on the Somerfeld pad near Dispersals in the grey light of the early dawn. She was charred and full of holes: it was the end of her flying days too; but she had held together and got us all home safely. I said a silent thank you to Barnes Wallis and the brilliance of his geodetic design and to the people at Vickers who had put her together.

After 15 bombing missions I was screened because, with my previous operations in Bomber Command and my flying hours in Coastal Command I had now completed two tours, that is the equivalent of 60 operational missions. By now it was 1944 and it should really have been the end of my front line flying but I managed to get a transfer back to Coastal Command and a posting to RAF Bircham Newton on the east coast in Norfolk. It was an Air Sea Rescue Squadron and my active flying could continue.

In addition to myself as pilot, my crew was a Navigator and a Wireless Operator/Air Gunner and our job was to fly out over the North Sea looking for survivors of any aircraft which had come down in the sea from the previous night's bombing raids. Our patrols were about four to five hour's duration. We flew Lockheed Hudsons, which were kitted out with dinghies and survival kits to drop to the aircrew in the water and some were even fitted with airborne lifeboats to drop.

On occasions we carried larger launches which were slung underneath the aircraft. We would drop these into the water close to the crews. Usually this was 'by request'; that is another aircraft, perhaps a Wellington, would have spotted the ditched crew and had radioed for assistance whilst it continued to circle the men awaiting our arrival. Dropping the launches or dinghies was fairly precise work since we had to get down low over the water, flying very slowly and drop them as close to the crews as possible but up-wind of them so that the craft would float to them and not away from them. The trick was to get the launch tight in on the crews without actually landing it on top of them. Once in the water, the launches could be unfolded in three sections and the engine started.

It is important to convey just how difficult it was to spot these crews as they drifted helplessly in the expanse of the North Sea. Their aircraft's rubber dinghy into which they had perhaps been able to climb, was only 6 feet across. The waves were often several feet high and so their chance of being seen from a ship was fairly slight; their main chance was to be seen from the air but a 6 foot rubber ring, no bigger than a tractor tyre, is a tiny object to spot from the air unless the aircraft flew very close and the crew were looking in the right place. Verey pistol flares played an important part in locating these men but many times it was a race between our own ASR launch and the Germans.

Ditching an aircraft into the sea was always a last resort because it was a manoeuvre fraught with danger. Ideally the aircraft should be ditched along the line of the waves rather than across them, to avoid ploughing into the water at 100mph or more, cartwheeling and breaking up. Often crew members were already wounded, the aircraft might sink quickly, although empty fuel tanks always helped buoyancy, and other injuries were often caused on impact when the crew were thrown about inside the fuselage; then there was the danger of getting caught up in the aerials and being dragged down with the 'plane, as happened to so many. Once outside the aircraft it was always best to try to get into the dinghy dry, but inevitably so many lads ended up in the water and had to climb in soaking wet. As the dinghy moved away from the stricken aircraft the surviving crew were exposed to the weather. Even in summer it was very cold, just not as cold as in winter. The spray from the waves would quickly deposit six or eight inches of water in the bottom of this rubber ring and the wind would cut through the airmen like a knife.

Our job was to find them as quickly as possible before the cold killed them or the Germans captured them – or machine-gunned them, as occasionally happened. Sometimes a crew had not been able to inflate their dinghy and were simply left bobbing about in the bitterly cold water, held up only by their Mae Wests. Their best chance of rescue came from tying themselves together to make a bigger target for us to see. On these occasions we would drop a covered dinghy so that at least they would be able to get out of the wind. We would then radio back their position whilst we circled overhead to give them protection against the enemy and to guide the rescue craft in.

Rescue came in many shapes and sizes including ASR launches, fishing boats, Royal Navy ships, flying boats and the enemy. To the men in the water, many of whom were also suffering from acute seasickness to add to their misery, it mattered not what it was only that it was rescue from an otherwise certain watery grave. British rescue was preferred but in the end rescue was rescue; even if a prison camp was the destination.

During my time on ASR we were responsible for the rescue of several bomber aircrews from the North Sea and it always gave us a great feeling of satisfaction to see these poor chaps being hauled to safety on a ship or boat. Once though I remember we spotted an empty dinghy being tossed around on the choppy water and although we searched until dark, we were unable to see any sign of the crew. That evening we returned to base feeling pretty low.

The German fighter attacked us from the setting sun and nearly blew us out of the sky. We were just finishing a square search looking for survivors when suddenly Jack, my WOP/AG, shouted through the intercom, "110 coming up fast, Skip". It had come at us from the west and Jack had only seen it at the last minute.

The Messerschmitt 110 was a two seater, twin-engine fighter not unlike a Stuka and although slower than the Me109, was still a lot faster than a Lockheed Hudson. The fighter fell upon us so quickly that Jack only had time to get off a short burst of fire, but it might well have been enough to spoil the pilot's aim. Almost at the same moment as I saw the black swastika crosses beneath its wings flash past my cockpit, I felt the Hudson lurch and tip over sharply to starboard. Our starboard engine had been hit and smoke was pouring out of it; we were out of control and heading straight into the North Sea.

Me110 - nearly the death of me

I knew that we had just one hope and as long as the Germans didn't come back we were just high enough for me to pull it off. Even though we were heading down towards the sea, I gave the port engine full throttle and opposite rudder to the failed engine. This had the effect of forcing the starboard wing to come up and sure enough we slowly started to come out of the dive and began to level off, correcting our drift to starboard. I had cut the fuel to the crippled engine and feathered the propellers so that they simply turned idly in the wind without causing any unnecessary drag. My mind flashed back to that raid on Essen a few months previously when a Me110 had almost shot me down that night. This one had done a better job than his countryman and though in serious trouble, we did still have a chance of survival. I was so glad that I had paid attention at Moose Jaw when the CFI had covered this recovery procedure in training.

Fortunately, the Luftwaffe crew had clearly decided that we were done for and had headed off home before darkness fell without coming back to check on us. We were now maintaining our height at about 200 feet above the sea but crabbing through the air. I asked Wally, the Navigator, for a course to our base at Bircham Newton and I slowly managed to get the Hudson to come round onto the course. I was in agony though because my calf muscles were getting cramp from the pressure of pressing my foot down on the rudder. I knew that I could not sustain this for much longer and my arms felt as if they were going to break from trying to hold the Hudson level.

Twin-engine aircraft are not designed to fly on one engine and so all the aerodynamics were pulling against me trying to turn the 'plane over. It was all those pressures and forces which I was fighting and I was losing the battle. I asked Wally to fetch the twine which I had seen at the back of the aircraft, to loop it around the right rudder and then pull like hell as if his life depended on it – because it did. What a relief it was when he took some of the pressure off me and how hard I prayed to see landfall: Anne Shelton has never sung a truer song, we really were coming home on a wing and a prayer. I knew that I was nearing the end of my strength but just then Wally shouted, "Coast line ahead. Don't let her go now Skipper." I looked through the fading light and there it was, land; although it was actually the waves crashing against the cliffs. My mouth was dry from the sheer exertion of fighting the controls and I croaked to Jack through the intercom to contact control and give them our position and tell them our problems. We crossed the coastline cliffs precariously low and were still crabbing badly but we were nearly home. I knew that we were at least going to come down on dry land but it was now all about how I got us down.

By map reading I could see we were over Hunstanton and we had been told to make for RAF Docking which was the Relief Landing Ground for our base and was about 3 miles away. I could still see the trail of smoke streaming out behind us from the starboard engine and leaving a lonely dark and ominous track across the still evening sky. I prayed that we did not catch fire now or we were done for. Wally released his hold on the twine and I took full control of the rudders. The pressure returned to my legs and the pain was excruciating. As we approached the airstrip the controller on the ground fired a green Verey light and then another. Thank God, that meant that we could go straight in and land. The hydraulics for the undercarriage were driven off the starboard engine so Jack, using our hand pump, laboriously lowered the wheels manually. I was now nearly in line for our approach and so throttling back I carried out a steep turn to the left. We were on our approach but far too high so with my nose in the air and nearly at stalling speed, with full opposite rudder I lost height rapidly, a manoeuvre I had luckily been taught by my initial training instructor in the early days at Dewinton. Holding her as steadily as I could I managed to come in just over the boundary hedge. I had no flaps and my wheels hit the Somerfeld tracking hard. The Hudson bounced and bounced again then finally landed on two wheels with quite a thud, but we were safely down. I switched off the port engine which had powered us home and the three of us hugged each other, just happy to be alive. After this mission I recommended both my crew members for awards.

For a few moments after the Me110 had shot us up, we all thought we would die as the Hudson had tipped over and headed for the cold waters of the North Sea. I was 10 years old again and drowning; all my holidays flashed across my mind as they had done that summer day in Shrewsbury 14 years earlier. The screaming noise of the Hudson as she plunged seawards, the words of my crew coming through my headset were all gone. It was quiet and serene in the cockpit as I saw my school holidays and waited for death. Then it was as if a light switched on in my brain and my trained reactions took over. The flying skills which I had been taught and had so diligently practised, together with some good luck, brought us home safely.

I was awarded the Distinguished Flying Cross for saving the lives of my crew and three days later there was a parade for immediate decoration by a Senior Officer from Group Headquarters. What a party we had both in the

Sergeants' Mess and the Officers' Mess.

My Distinguished Flying Cross

I remember my CO, Wing Commander Luscombe, placing his arms around me and congratulating me on my courage and a fine piece of airmanship. He knew how easy it would have been for me to order the crew to bale out and all the risks which that involved. But as so often in war we moved on and shortly afterwards I was posted to RAF Upavon on a Pilot Instructor's course. This was the 'Top Gun' Academy of its day. I had by now completed a third tour of operational flying, 90 missions and that was enough. I was considered to be among the best of the best and was being trained to teach the best of the rest.

Chapter 11

Top Gun

I arrived at RAF Upavon for an extensive course of flying and the twin-engine Airspeed Oxfords were the training aircraft once more. My instructor taught me the skills of providing a running commentary of all my movements whilst flying; it was called 'patter'. The patter from the instructor was the same as it had been at Condover, on my first Advanced Flying Course. It became quite an art but it was surprising how it made much better pilots of us; I could practically fly the Oxford blindfolded. Happily I passed out from the course with above average marks; this was a prerequisite for an instructor at the Advanced Flying School.

I was posted to 15(P) AFU [Advanced Flying Unit] at Castle Combe in Wiltshire. The Chief Flying Instructor was an old Squadron Leader who had seen service in the First World War. He wore a scruffy uniform with his 1914-18 medals and had eyes so pink and bleary above very large dark bags that I couldn't believe he could find the cockpit of an aeroplane, never mind fly it. In fact pre-war, he had been a pilot in Cobham's Air Circus. After the First World War ended, many pilots leaving the newly formed Royal Air Force turned to stunt work to earn a living. The aircraft then were all slow but very manoeuvrable bi-planes which were ideal for that kind of work. A lot of these chaps were happy to see the war come again because it gave them employment and the opportunity to fly the new breed of aircraft that I had grown up with. Later, when I was made PMC of the mess I found out the cause of the pink eyes – too many pink gins!

I had been posted to Castle Combe as Flight Commander and the next morning, driving my open top MG TA which I had bought two years before, I arrived at 'Q' Flight. I met my team of nine instructors who over the next few months would be my right hand men. Actually they all had far more experience of instructing than I did, which was not difficult because I had none at all. Nevertheless we pulled together and became a great team. Two of the team though were particularly fine instructors; Flying Officer Paul Kemp, who was soon made up to Flight Lieutenant and Flight Sergeant Honey, whom I recommended for a commission and happily on his promotion stayed with me on the Flight.

Castle Combe was great fun because I was still able to fly. Not long after my arrival, by one of those happy coincidences in life, I was seconded to the Empire Central Flying School at RAF Hullavington for a fortnight as OC Night Flying. When I got there I spotted a single engine bi-plane parked up quietly not far from the Control Tower; it was a little Auster. A couple of nights later I met the Station CO in the Mess and asked him if I could borrow the Auster when I went back to Castle Combe at the end of my secondment. "Of course Ted, help yourself" and so Paul Kemp, my Number 2, flew me over to pick her up. I enjoyed many hours in that little Auster flying it around, looping the loop, barrel rolling and so on. This is what I had joined the RAF for back in 1939 and what was so lovely about it now was that for the first time in 5 years, no-one was trying to shoot me out of the sky. I kept the Auster though for rather longer than the CO had probably had in mind when he said "help yourself" because she was still at Castle Combe when I flew out of the base as the last serving Officer to do so, well after the war had finished. Sadly, the new owners of the airfield had no affection for her and they dug a hole in the ground with one of the new JCBs and just bulldozed her into it. Such a waste, but not untypical of the times.

By this stage of the war we knew that we were going to win; it was no longer a case of if, but when. D-Day had happened and the Allies were pushing across Europe. We were not really told of the calamity that was Arnhem. The events that had conspired to prevent the capture of the bridge, despite the exemplary courage of the British 1st Airborne Division under the command of General Roy Urquhart, put an end to hopes that the war would be over by Christmas 1944, but the eventual outcome was never in doubt. The British war cemetery at Arnhem is testimony to the sacrifice of so many, including twins from the Staffordshire Regiment who joined together, had consecutive Service numbers and were killed on September 19th within hours of each other.

At Castle Combe we knew nothing of this; we had fought hard and survived so far; life was still for living as if each day was our last. I was young, free and single, I had an MG sports car and a gallantry medal on my chest: the girls loved it and I loved them. The world was a very different place and we did things then that we could not do today. Paul Kemp and I would have a few beers in the Officers' Mess and then jump into my car and drive to the village pub where we would have a few more and meet up with some girls. The four of us would then get into the two-seater MG and go on to another pub and so on.

At the time, my brother Len held the rank of Major in the KSLI and was stationed at Copthorne Barracks in Shrewsbury. One Friday morning with a bicycle in the back of an Oxford aircraft, I flew up to Shropshire and landed at RAF Montford Bridge, about three miles north of the town. I cycled home to mum and dad's from where I telephoned Len at the barracks and he joined us for lunch. In the afternoon we both cycled back to Montford Bridge airfield, loaded our bikes into the Oxford and took off for RAF Castle Combe where Len joined us in the Mess for an Officers' social evening.

The next day we left the Base and I flew Len back to RAF Montford Bridge. As a navigation aid, I followed the main Wolverhampton to Shrewsbury railway line, but as we neared Wellington we ran into thick cloud and so I climbed to 4,000 feet to get above it. At that height we came out into brilliant sunshine but there was no hole in the cloud for me to find Montford Bridge airfield. The cloud ceiling was completely flat and stretched as far as I could see. The clouds were pure white in the dazzling sunlight and I thought back to that night returning from

Essen when my Wellington bomber had been silhouetted by the moonlight above a similar carpet of cloud. This time though I could enjoy the splendour of the scene without worrying about German fighters – there weren't any within 600 miles of us and I felt very contented. Len clearly did not share my contentment and was getting agitated about how we were ever going to get down safely through the cloud. I contacted RAF Shawbury on the R/T and they gave me a magnetic course to their airfield from which I was able to fly through the dense cloud. Len, who of course couldn't hear any of this radio guidance, was convinced that I was flying 'blind' through the clouds and grew increasingly concerned as we gradually lost height. In due course we came out of the clouds again around 500 feet above Shawbury. It was then a straightforward matter to fly to Montford Bridge and land safely. Poor Len, once more unimpressed by his younger brother's antics, swore that he would never fly with me ever again.

On an earlier trip up to Shrewsbury, I had put a dozen 'Bronco' lavatory rolls into the Oxford and then Len and I flew over our parents' house, which was by then off the Roman Road, and coming down dangerously low we used the rolls to bomb mum and dad whilst they sat in the garden. On another occasion I beat up the barracks at Copthorne. The squaddies were all on parade and again I flew so low over the parade ground that they dived in all directions to take cover. Len was not amused when he heard about this incident because he knew that this would be my doing.

Whenever a complaint was made about these pranks and the complainant had got the number from the fuselage of my aircraft, I got away with it because they all thought that I was suffering from battle fatigue after having done 90 Ops. That number of Ops certainly did affect me, but I milked it and although the grizzly old Squadron Leader CFI didn't like me, the Group Captain did and they left me alone. In any case the CFI was too busy getting gin into himself and a particular WAAF into his quarters.

Every two months we rotated from daylight flying to night flying and I was made Officer Commanding Night Flying. It was on one of these nights that my life was to change. I stood near the bar in the Officers' Mess drinking half a pint of shandy and chatting with our Medical Officer. I told him I was just leaving to go to the Flights to carry out a weather check and asked if he had ever flown at night before. He told me that he hadn't and so I invited him to come along for the ride. We piled into the MG and drove over to the Flights.

It was about eight o' clock on a cold, wet, starless, pitch dark February evening. In 1945 there was none of the sophisticated computerised weather forecasting gadgetry of today: if you wanted to know how high the cloud base was, you took off and kept going up until you ran into the stuff. Simple.

My routine was as usual: as OC Night Flying I met everyone who would be flying that night, instructors and pupil pilots alike, explained the weather conditions for the night as I had been given it by the Met boys, outlined the aerial activities at RAF Lyneham and RAF Hullavington, our neighbouring airfields and explained the navigational cross country flights for the night exercises. I then asked for questions. After this I called at the Flight office, met Paul Kemp and booked myself out with the MO as my passenger.

We clambered up into the Airspeed Oxford and I went through the take-off procedure. We taxied along the perimeter track, carried out further take-off checks and contacted the control tower on the R/T to ask for permission to take off. I watched for the green light from the control cabin at the start of the runway and I slowly turned onto the paraffin gooseneck flare path. I lined up the aircraft, opened both throttles and we started to roll forward. She slowly gathered speed and as we powered down the strip I eased the wheel slightly and she lifted effortlessly off the ground. At about thirty feet into the air I raised my undercarriage and kept her at full power as we started to climb away from the airfield. I glanced at the MO sitting beside me in the co-pilot's seat and he had a boyish grin on his face as the excitement of his first night flight began.

I had no sooner thought, "I'm glad the MO is enjoying this; he'll remember tonight all his life", when the whole aircraft suddenly began to shake violently; I could hardly hold the wheel. The starboard engine was failing but still producing power on full revs. We were barely fifty feet off the ground and I knew that if I didn't shut down the engine the aircraft would just break up in the air under the strain and violence of the vibrations. The trouble was that once I shut the engine down, the Oxford would flip over and crash anyway. Well I had done it once before when the Me110 shot us up, but that time I had a lot more air underneath me to start with than the fifty feet I had now.

I had no choice though and I shut down the engine; but even as I applied full power to the port engine and opposite rudder to the failed starboard one, the aircraft swung violently to starboard and headed straight for the houses of Castle Combe. In that moment I was sure that this was the end but I knew that I had to pull us clear of the village first. I looked up from the instrument panel just in time to see the steeple of the village church looming out of the darkness straight in front of us. It flashed by with no more than inches to spare and to this day I don't know how we didn't hit it. I was maintaining height and even gaining a little, but where was I going; I was flying into complete darkness. The near miss on the steeple had at least given me an idea of my location and height; I was at about a hundred feet and clear of the houses: the families of Castle Combe were safe. Now I needed to try and save our own lives.

I was pressing hard on the left rudder and crabbing badly through the air: there was more than a touch of deja vous about this little lot. Desperate for help, I contacted the control tower on the R/T. I told the duty WAAF controller that I needed to make a 'pukka' single engine landing and explained to her the problems I had.

In those days 'pukka' had nothing to do with cooking but was code for, 'this is a real emergency, not an exercise'. I put on my navigation lights and asked the WAAF to try and guide us back to the airfield.

I heard her quiet, calm and efficient voice from out of the ether in my headset, "Yes Charlie Juliet, I can see you now. Turn to port about 45 degrees. You should see the flare path. Suggest you then turn ninety degrees to port Charlie Juliet." I knew that in the control tower all attention would be focused on this one young woman. The only sounds to break the silence would be the voice of this WAAF as she sat in front of her R/T set and the gas light suspended from the ceiling, turned down low and quietly hissing from its mantle, casting a warm yellow glow around the room. Her voice betrayed no sign of alarm or flap and I was greatly encouraged by that fact: I knew that she had trained for this sort of emergency and I just hoped to God that she was up to it. If ever I needed help it was now. My great problem was that I just could not get the aircraft high enough for me to see the flare path and I needed this WAAF, who I knew could see my navigation lights, to talk me round over the fields and trees back to the end of the airstrip.

My arms were aching and the pressure on my legs was unbearable. I suddenly remembered my passenger and glanced across at the MO. He was as white as a sheet and frozen to his seat with fear. He couldn't speak and from the cockpit instrument lights I could see that had he lost control of his bladder. He needed something to do and I had just the job for him. God must have been with me that night because had I not had the MO on board I would have been unable to lower the undercarriage and a crash landing with full fuel tanks would have been awaiting me; like the Lockheed Hudson, the undercarriage of the Airspeed Oxford was powered by the starboard engine.

I carried on someway down my downwind leg and shouted to the MO to pump like hell on the lever I showed him, which would lower our undercarriage. "Control to

Charlie Juliet, you need to turn ninety degrees to port." It was that clear, calm voice again reminding me that we were not alone. "You should be able to see the flare path any time now". I acknowledged her instructions and turned crosswind and then turned onto my landing approach. "Come in Charlie Juliet, you're too low on your approach", and to my horror I was in red on my glide path indicator; there were some cottages about a hundred yards from the airfield boundary and I was about to land on top of them. I just managed to keep enough height to somehow stay above them and then the green colour showed up on the glide indicator. Within seconds I thankfully throttled back on my port engine and took full control of the aircraft with both rudders. I glided over the boundary fence and saw the crash wagon, ambulance and the Station fire engine racing towards us. The Senior Controller stood outside his cabin watching what was happening. In all the circumstances it was a perfect landing and we ran to the end of the goosenecks nearly colliding with our welcoming party. I switched off the port engine and turned to shake hands with the MO. Still shaking and in need of a clean pair of pants, "Ted," he said, "I may be in the RAF but that is the first and last time I ever want to fly." I smiled and thought of my brother Len's words in much the same vein. It was all part of the excitement of flying in those days and I had seen it all before.

We were taken to the Flights by the crash wagon where Paul, who had heard from the Control Tower that we had landed safely, had two large mugs of hot tea waiting for us on his desk. Paul then phoned for the Station car to take the MO back to his billet; as he left all I could say to him was "Sorry old boy". The next half an hour was spent giving Paul the details of what had happened so that he could fill in his Night Diary.

Paul offered me another cup of tea, but I had something else on my mind; I walked over to the Control Tower and asked the Senior Controller which young WAAF had helped me down. He pointed to a hatch in the corner of the room and said, "Through there, Sir." I walked across the room and opened the hatch door; there, sitting in front of their radios were four young WAAFs. I pushed my cap to the back of my head and leaned in saying, "Which one of you helped me to land?" Blushingly, the prettiest one said, "I did, Sir". She was stunning, by far the most beautiful girl I had ever seen. I had a picture in my mind of how lovely this girl would be from the voice which I had heard through my headset, but I was not prepared for the beauty who was looking at me now. I thanked her very much and told them all I that would send them a box of chocolates. Quite where I was going to get a box of chocolates from in wartime Wiltshire, I did not know but still, the thought was there.

The next afternoon I reported to my Senior Officer, the Squadron Leader CFI with the liking for pink gin. He had the report in front of him about my fun and games the night before. The inspection of the aircraft had shown that a piece of one of the propellers, which were wooden, had sheared off and that had thrown the whole balance of the engine out of true and had caused the violent vibrations. The CFI said he was going to recommend me for an award and although I really didn't like the fellow, I shook hands with him and left. It was some days later and at the end of the month when my logbook was returned to me signed by the CFI; this was a monthly duty to confirm flying hours. Turning to the back page there was my award for saving the life of the Station MO and securing one of His Majesty's aircraft – a piece of paper pasted in on the back cover. It was called a Green Endorsement, written in longhand with green ink congratulating me on my airmanship that night, signed and dated by the Group Captain. I have always thought that my airmanship in that incident was far more demanding and the circumstances more dangerous because of the lack of height and the proximity of the village houses and church, than my previous single engine episode; but who am I to argue with a circus flier?

That night I was on night flying duty again and I made a point of visiting the Control Tower, this time before I took off. I had been thinking about that WAAF all day and I could not get her face out of my mind; I knew that I had to see her. This time I went into their room and sitting with them, shared a cup of coffee. Sure enough my chance came and I whispered to her to step out of the room; there, in the outer office I asked her out for dinner. She accepted straight away. My heart was beating far faster then than it had been the night before when I thought I was going to die and I wondered if she could see how excited I was.

LAC Joy Worthington

We were both off duty the following night so met a few yards from her billet, but on the main road outside the camp. She jumped into my MG and covered herself with the car blanket; this was 1945 and other ranks were not allowed to socialise with Officers. We drove to a hotel in Chippenham, some ten miles away, and spent a marvellous evening together. Her name was Joy Worthington. She was very different from the other girls I had dated. Joy had been born and brought up in Cornwall and after leaving school, her family had moved to Bristol where she had worked as a secretary. One morning in 1944 she set off for work as usual but as she turned the corner of the street where she worked, her office block was no longer there; it had been bombed in the night and she was out of work. She joined the WAAFs and later that year was posted to RAF Castle Combe. She was stunningly good looking, quiet and kind, good humoured and good fun. She was never short of a date and I couldn't believe I was taking her out.

We carried on seeing each other through the Spring and by May I knew that I had to ask her. After six years of war I was more accustomed to giving orders than to asking pretty WAAFs to marry me; I hadn't done this sort of thing before. So one warm, still evening at the beginning of May, a few days before the war ended, I took Joy out for a ride in the MG through the gentle Wiltshire countryside. We could feel the fields and hedges around us breathing a sigh of relief that peace was almost here; that the roar of engines and the chatter of machine guns were coming to an end. The rays of the early evening sun were still warm as they cast long shadows across the winding country lanes. The first swallows dipped low over the water meadows and fields of waving hay. It was comforting to know that despite the carnage which the human race had visited upon itself, the rhythm of nature remained undisturbed. This year these heralds of an English summer would also herald peace. We knew that we had won the war; it was now a matter of waiting for the inevitability of the Nazis' final surrender.

But I was not at peace. My insides were churning. This was more nerve racking than any bombing raid over Germany: what if she said "No"? We went to The Cat and Fiddle, the little country pub we had been to so often, had a couple of drinks and a meal and then headed back towards the airfield. I looked at her sitting beside me in the car; her uniform clipping the slim shape of her body, her head thrown back and the wind blowing through her hair. She was beautiful. I had to ask her now. I pulled the car into a field gateway and we got out and walked a short way hand in hand without speaking. Presently we stopped and kissed long and passionately, leaning against the old gatepost that had hosted so many lovers over so many years. It had to be now I thought. The moment was so right. I had to ask her now. I held her close and whispered the words I had practised all week. "Yes", she said, "you know I will".

Joy and I alongside the aircraft that brought us together

Well, Joy had accepted me but I still needed to meet her father and ask him for permission to marry his daughter. I don't suppose though that this courtesy is required of today's generation. We travelled to Chippenham in Gloucestershire were I met Reg Worthington. He was a delightful man who had lost his right leg in a harrowing accident involving a threshing machine and now walked with an artificial limb. Agricultural accidents of this sort were not uncommon at the time; the Health and Safety Executive would have been horrified by many of the working practices which were simply taken then as normal routine. Once more my heart was pounding as I asked Mr Worthington for his daughter's hand. I can still remember my intense relief and excitement when he said, "Yes Ted, I would be delighted for Joy to marry you". That night I telephoned my mother to tell her the news; on reflection I think I should have told her to sit down first because I could tell that she was somewhat surprised. By now I was 25 and hadn't really settled with a steady girlfriend before yet here I was, her youngest son, telling her that I was soon to be married. When she had gathered her breath again she bubbled with excitement, "What's her name, Edward? When are you going to bring her home to meet us?" "This weekend, all being well", I replied.

The down side of being a pilot is that if the plane is going to crash it is your duty to save the life of your crew before saving your own life: I had learnt that over the Bay of Biscay in 1940. On the plus side, on the ground, there are some advantages. We needed to get up to Shrewsbury to see my parents and then back to Castle Combe. After all, Britain was still at war and we were both still in the RAF with a job to do. So I used my rank and issued Joy with a 48-hour pass, that is, leave the Base on Friday evening and be back at 23.59 hours on Sunday. We got away on Friday and travelled to Shrewsbury in the MG where mum and dad met Joy with open arms and welcomed her to the family. No doubt both my parents were more than a little relieved that at last I had shown signs of settling down but probably had some pity for Joy.

In the evening we walked to our local pub, the Beacon in Copthorne Road and I introduced Joy to a Flight Lieutenant friend Bob Love, who was the Equipment Officer at RAF Shawbury. Little did he know that night that he would have to step in at literally a moment's notice to be my best man.

We had a lovely time that weekend. Len was still at Copthorne Barracks and so on the Saturday night Len, Joy and I went out into Shrewsbury. We went around all our old haunts; I was so proud of Joy and introduced her to everyone I knew. Poor Joy she couldn't possibly have remembered everyone's name. Len came up to our parents' house for Sunday lunch and my sister, who was nursing all through the war, was there too. After a quiet walk in the afternoon Joy and I set off back to RAF Castle Combe before her 48-hour pass ran out. Shrewsbury to Castle Combe doesn't seem far today but in 1945 there were no motorways and even the major roads were fairly narrow. It took us about 6 hours to get back. Not all of that was travelling of course; we stopped along the way for a drink and a bite to eat and, well we just stopped along the way!

Chapter 12
Peace and Matrimony

Hitler was rumoured to be dead and there was now a real sense that the war in Europe would soon be over, and so it was. The next day, on the morning of Monday 7th May 1945 the Officers' Mess was bustling with expectation as we gathered around the Marconi wireless set which sat on the table in the corner. Churchill was about to broadcast to the Nation and we all knew the words which we wanted to hear from the great man.

"Yesterday morning at 2.41am, at General Eisenhower's Headquarters, General Jodel, the representative of the German High Command and of Grand Admiral Donitz the designated Head of the German State, signed the act of unconditional surrender of all German land, sea and air forces in Europe, to the Allied Expeditionary Force and simultaneously to the Soviet High Command... ..Today this agreement will be ratified and confirmed at Berlin. Hostilities will end officially at one minute after midnight tonight, Tuesday 8th May......"

Winston Spencer Churchill, British Prime Minister. Monday 7th May 1945.

For a few seconds after Churchill had finished speaking we were all silent, and then a great cheer went up. We had made it; we really had won the war, in Europe at least. Five years ago in May 1940 after Dunkirk, no one really gave Britain a hope against the might of the Third Reich. But we had come through it victorious and those of us standing there had lived to see this day. The bar was open and in a moment of solemnity we raised a glass to all our comrades who had died to make this victory possible. The war was to have cost the lives of 305,000 British Servicemen and women.

Churchill had declared Tuesday 8th and Wednesday 9th May as days of celebration and celebrate we certainly did. A large bonfire was built near the Airmen's Mess and now, with complete disregard for the protocol of Officers and other ranks mixing, I drove up to the WAAFs' billet in my MG to collect Joy. She was after all now my fiancée. I called at the back of the Officer's Mess, I wasn't quite so blasé as to turn up at the front door with Joy in the car, and collected a bottle of Bells whisky from the bar. I slipped it into the glove compartment and we drove over to the Flights where I picked up my Flight Sergeant, two mechanics and a Corporal. All crammed into the open top sports car, we drove to one of our favourite local pubs in Castle Combe, the Castle Inn. The ecstatic scenes of pleasure were something the likes of which I haven't seen since. Five years earlier we had been expecting the Nazis to roll over the English Channel and occupy our Country. Now we were free of that threat. As a Nation, we have had nothing to compare with that sense of relief since then. People were laughing and screaming with pure delight that it was all over. In addition to the locals, the whole Squadron seemed to be present and by 11o' clock we had drunk the Castle Inn dry. We sang all the usual RAF songs and out on the car park couples were laughing and kissing and inevitably letting their inhibitions fall away; it was going to be a long night, so we piled back into my car and set off for the Base.

As we drove through Castle Combe village my Flight Sergeant suddenly shouted, "Stop!" I thought we had lost someone over the back of the car but instead he stood up and with his .22 air rifle tried to shoot the weathercock off the top of the church tower. He was far too drunk and despite having several shots couldn't get a hit. I told him that he was hopeless and that I had got closer with the wing of my Oxford the night the MO had nearly died of fright. Amid the ensuing laughter I let out the clutch of the MG a bit quickly and nearly left the Flight Sergeant sitting on the road, which entertained us even more.

I parked the MG at the back of the Officers' Mess, and after checking that the Bells was still in the glove compartment, Joy and I walked to the All Ranks' dance in the Airmen's Mess. The celebrations were in full swing here too. The Station band was playing Glenn Miller's *In the Mood* and other American dance tunes which we had come to know and love over the last five years; everyone was up on their feet, there was hardly room to swing a cat round never mind to jitterbug. Joy and I were dancing when the Station Warrant Officer climbed on a table and announced that Flight Lieutenant Cowling was about to light the bonfire. I held Joy's hand as we went outside but in the crush we got separated and lost each other. Well, duty comes first and so I carried on to the bonfire, only to find it already burning furiously thanks to a drunken erk with a box of matches. I went back to the Airmen's Mess to look for Joy but I couldn't find her anywhere. I wandered around for about an hour, bumping into people I knew and having drinks thrust into my hand. Oh well I thought, she is quite capable of looking after herself and has probably gone back to her billet. It was now 3 o' clock in the morning; I decided to call it a night and walked back to my car. As I got close I heard laughter and saw two people sitting in the car drinking my Scotch. It was Joy and Flight Lieutenant Robinson, a friend of mine whom we called Robbo. I thought that was pretty mean of a chap; I didn't mind him chatting up my girl but drinking my whisky was a different matter altogether!

They were clearly both enjoying themselves so I left them to it. I was tired now and the evening had caught up with me but by not disturbing Joy and Robbo I had lost my transport, so I set off to walk back to my billet about 3 miles away across the airfield. I walked over towards the bonfire which was still burning brightly but as I turned away from it I was momentarily blinded and walked into a wire fence. Ah! The main road I thought and I climbed through the fence, only to fall head first into the static water tank which was some 20 feet deep. Luckily it had been topped up that day and so I was able to cling to the side and haul myself out. What a sorry state I was in but it certainly sobered me up quickly. Fortunately everyone else, apart from the poor souls on sentry duty, were too drunk to notice a wet, bedraggled and shivering Flight Lieutenant plodding his way across the airfield to his billet.

Life was pretty good now. The war in Europe was over, although it would continue in the Far East for another 3 months until the atomic bombs on Hiroshima and Nagasaki on 6th and 9th August finally sank the Rising Sun of the Imperial Japanese Empire. Joy and I met most nights and we would go out for a drive or to a pub for a drink and a meal. One evening we drove to The White Swan, a pub near Filton just outside Bristol, at least it was outside Bristol in 1945. We had a lovely meal despite the rationing which would continue for several years yet. When we got back to Castle Combe Joy realised that she had left her handbag in the pub. This was very serious of course because not only did it contain Joy's money and personal items, it also held her Identity papers. If she lost those then she would be on a serious charge.

So the next day I telephoned the licensee at The White Swan and asked him if anyone had found Joy's handbag. "Yes sir, we have LAC Worthington's handbag here. One of our customers found it last night just after you had gone. We'll keep it safe until you can come and collect it." Filton was about 20 miles away and it would take me too long to drive over and get it so I asked the licensee if there was a field nearby where I could land an aeroplane and collect the bag from him. "Oh yes," he said, "just next to us. The fellows from Filton often land in the field to come here." I thanked him and told him that I was on my way. I had a quick word with Paul Kemp and booked my Oxford out for an instrument test. 15 minutes later I touched down in the field next to The White Swan, and leaving my engines running, I dashed into the pub and collected Joy's bag. I thanked the landlord and gave him a shilling [5p in today's money] and asked him to buy a drink for whomever it was that had handed in Joy's bag. As I ran out of the door back to the 'plane I heard him call after me, "My word sir, she must be very special. I hope she appreciates it." I was up and away in double quick time and back to Base post haste before anyone had missed me. This little escapade could have had me court martialled if ever it had been found out. What we do for love. That night I gave Joy her handbag. She was so relieved and asked me how I had got it. I just gave her a big kiss and held her tightly. She knew exactly how I had got it – and she was very appreciative.

On Bomber Command we had enjoyed the company of Flying Officer The Hon. Stanley Malpass, Bt., and here on Training Command we had our share of nobility too. The Station Adjutant was Flight Lieutenant Abel-Smith, whom it was rumoured was not too distantly related to Royalty, for his family were extensive landowners in Herefordshire and there was a Royal connection somewhere there. He spoke like Prince Charles, had as little to do with us aircrew types as possible and kept himself to himself.

Abel-Smith lived in the same nissen hut as the permanent members of staff but he didn't associate with us at all. Our hut was about three miles from the Officers' Mess and he drove around the Base in a magnificent black Rolls-Royce. The window of his room looked straight across the main road and he parked his Rolls outside this window and I would park my MG either in front or behind the Rolls, depending upon which one of us came in last – usually me. On the other side of the road and opposite his bedroom window was a gate which was kept locked with a chain and padlock. Beyond the gate there was a newly built hayrick.

One night in the Officers' Mess we hatched a plan to set Abel-Smith up and so after he had gone to bed, complete with silk pyjamas and cravat, we lifted the gate off its hinges and pushed the Rolls across the road and into the field up to the hayrick. Of course at that time no one ever thought of locking their car or taking the keys out. We then dismantled the hayrick, moved the car a few more feet and rebuilt the hayrick on top of the car. By the time we had finished, tidied up the site and removed all trace of hay from our clothes, it had taken us nearly four hours; we had just finished before the dawn broke.

At 10.00 hours that morning three detectives visited the Flight Office to interview me: was the Rolls there when I drove my MG away at 08.00? "Yes, it certainly was, because I had had to reverse and drive around it to get out"; had I seen anything suspicious? "No, I had not", and so on. Eventually they went away satisfied that I was unable to help them with their enquiries any further. Wiltshire Police searched the county for Abel-Smith's Rolls for 14 days but didn't find it. After that we took pity on him having to use Base transport and dropped an anonymous note into the police station in Chippenham saying where the Rolls could be found. In due course two Police cars arrived and several officers set about dismantling the hayrick, whilst Abel-Smith stood to one side with the senior detective. It was all too good a show for us to miss: the five of us who had pulled the prank stood by the gate, caps tipped back and hands in our pockets as the rick was slowly taken apart; sure enough there was the Rolls. Inside the car was a note which said, "Hello, fancy seeing you here". Abel-Smith was furious, but of course he couldn't prove that we were responsible although he knew very well that we were. The Chief Constable, who was a retired Brigadier, was even less impressed with his detectives than Abel-Smith was with our prank, but the CO let it slip in the Mess one night that the Chief Constable considered it to be an internal RAF matter. We heard nothing more about it.

12th July 1945 was the date Joy and I had set for our wedding and it was fast approaching. I had arranged to fly Joy to Theale airfield near Reading to stay with her Aunt for the few days before our wedding. Flying Joy to Theale without good reason was against the rules. The RAF was not a private taxi firm for its pilots' love lives, even if we did sometimes use it as that.

I had also arranged for my barman to order the drinks for the wedding through the Officers' Mess bar so that I could buy it all at cost price. Although this was not at all illegal, it was against the Mess rules, so not only was I going to be flying an unauthorised WAAF passenger, I would also be carrying a very large 'grip' full of unauthorised booze. Everything was ready and we were about to go across to the waiting 'plane when I had a telephone call from Group Captain Robinson at RAF Babdown Farm, our parent unit. "Ah Ted, I understand that you are flying to Theale. That will suit me just fine, as I have to catch a train from Reading to London. Pick me up please". "Yes Sir", I said; God, now what was I to do; the WAAF, the booze...oh well too late now I thought. One good thing anyway, at least the CO has made this into an authorised flight to Theale.

I picked Joy up with her luggage together with my heavy grip of booze and drove to the Flights; we took off for the 15 miles hop to RAF Babdown Farm where the Group Captain was waiting. I taxied to the control tower and as the 'plane came to a standstill an airman opened the door and the CO got in. Joy was sitting next to me in the pupil's seat; the CO scowled and said, "Come on WAAF, I'm sitting there", and poor Joy ended up sitting on the hard member between the two seats with no harness to hold her in. We took off again and landed at Theale not long after. I taxied the Oxford around as close to the Guard Room as I could safely get it and Joy and the CO clambered out. But Joy was struggling with her two very heavy cases, inside one of which the bottles were chinking together and making an awful noise. "Come here WAAF, let me help you," said the CO and taking my grip with all the wedding booze inside from her, he set off towards the Guard Room. If he takes that in there I thought, there will be no wedding never mind no wedding booze. Good old Joy; before they got close enough for the duty Military Policeman to hear the chinking, she took over and walked to the entrance of the RAF Station hoping to get a lift from a passing motorist. A woman could do that with safety in 1945, especially one in uniform.

Well, I could do no more for her now, so I taxied back to the runway and took off again to return to RAF Castle Combe. Before heading back though I circled the field to see if Joy had got a lift; she certainly had but I could hardly believe what I saw. The CO's staff car pulled out of the Station gates where the sentries stood smartly to attention; barely ten yards down the road it stopped beside Joy and after a brief conversation I saw the CO's driver get out of the car and whilst Joy got into the front passenger seat, he put her two bags into the boot. The CO had asked her where she was going to and when she said, "Reading Sir", he had told her to jump in. Joy rode in style all the way to Reading Station, some 8 miles, with the Group Captain's pendant flying on the bonnet of the car and for the second time in as many months I saw my fiancé sitting in a car with another man and my booze disappearing with them!

Now that peace had broken out across Europe the War Department knowing what we didn't, that atomic weapons were very soon to be used against Japan to end the war in the Pacific, wasted no time in dismantling the infrastructure which had served us so well. RAF Castle Combe was to be closed down and the whole unit was scheduled for transfer to RAF Brize Norton.

Well that would be that, but before I left I wanted to have one last flight in the old Auster. The mechanic wound the propeller, the engine fired as sweetly as it always did and away I went far up into the Wiltshire sky. For over an hour I played in that cherished little bi-plane; doing aerobatics in her was such a luxury. Throughout the war I had flown many types of aircraft from bi-planes to Wellington bombers but I had never flown a sweeter, kinder aeroplane than that little Auster.

I looped the loop, barrelled rolled and simply wallowed in the exhilaration of the open cockpit, the clear blue sky reaching high above me and the patchwork of the green and yellow fields of England stretched out far below me. I can still remember the raw, naked pleasure of that day and am reminded of the first and last lines of "High Flight", that wonderful pilots' poem by John Gillespie Magee who was so tragically killed in an aerial collision over RAF Cranwell whilst flying his Spitfire on 11 December 1941. He was just 19 years of age.

"Oh, I have slipped the surly bonds of earth......

Put out my hand, and touched the face of God."

Finally and sadly, it was time to land but before I did I would beat up the Station for one last time. I dived in towards the buildings but as I started the roll I knew I was too low; the little Auster though responded to my most delicate of touches and she pulled us out and away; wow, was I ever so high on adrenalin! I could have stayed and stayed but my fuel gauge told me it was time to call it a day and I came back down to earth.

We closed the doors on RAF Castle Combe and together with my nine instructors, we flew the ten Airspeed Oxfords into RAF Brize Norton in formation. If nothing else we would show this lot how the Advanced Flying School did things; the CO was tipped off about our formation arrival and told me in the Mess later that he had actually been rather impressed but not to make a habit of it!

Airspeed Oxford

It was 11th July when I booked into the hotel in Reading with my mother, father, sister, Robert Love, Maidi his wife and Joy's father. We had a riotous evening which included me taking off Reg Worthington's shirt and trousers and stealing his wooden leg. We passed it around and somehow lost it in the drunken melee. Poor man, he had to hop to bed that night but he took it all in good spirits and saw the funny side of it. Thinking back, it was a disgraceful thing to do but very funny at the time. Len, who was supposed to be my best man, had still not turned up by the end of the evening.

The Church of England wedding service next day was at Christ Church, Reading. The church stood at the top of a very steep bank and we were all assembled awaiting Joy's arrival. Her relations were there together with my own and many of my fellow Officers from the Station; but where was my best man? We waited and we waited, but still no Len. I knew that Joy would be on her way by now so I walked over to Robert Love and asked him to stand in as my best man; fortunately I had the ring, not Len. Just in time Bob joined me at the front as Joy and her father, now reunited with his artificial leg, together with Joy's sister Pat, sadly no longer with us, and my own sister as Bridesmaids, entered the Church. It was a lovely service and Joy was a vision of beauty; I felt like the luckiest man in the world.

I had booked our honeymoon at the White Hart Hotel at Blackmoor Gate which lies between Linton and Lynmouth. My little sports car wasn't really big enough for the two of us and all our kit, so I borrowed Joy's uncle's Rover and as we pulled up to the front door all the other guests in the hotel were watching us through the windows; they knew we were a honeymoon couple. We were greeted by the owner who kindly gave us a bottle of champagne to enjoy with our dinner after which we went up to bed. In our room I drew the curtains, at least I tried to; they had been glued to the window and wouldn't budge. Never mind, we turned the light out and got into bed only to find an 'apple pie bed' waiting for us. There was nothing for it, we had to strip it back and make it again. It wasn't quite how I had imagined my honeymoon starting but it was fun and we have had many a good laugh about it over the years.

Our wedding day - 12th July 1945

After our honeymoon we returned to Reading and stayed with Joy's aunt for a few days. Joy's uncle said that he had liked the MG but had found it a bit awkward to get in and out of. Her aunt had simply refused to go in it a second time after she had exposed all her underwear trying to clamber out of it. She didn't know how Joy managed to get in and out all the time and still retain her modesty! We took our leave of them and thanked them for all their help and, back in the MG, we returned to RAF Brize Norton and lived in bed and breakfast accommodation as there were no married quarters available to us.

At the end of July 1945 the Station Group Captain set up a demob board to talk to airmen about civilian life and the options available to them in Civvy Street. I was appointed as Staff Officer to the Group Captain, promoted to Squadron Leader and given a seat on the demob board. Although this was quite interesting at first it soon became tedious and repetitive. However one advantage of all this inactivity was that Joy and I had more time to spend together. We enjoyed the money which my promotion had brought and, although there were still several years of austerity ahead of us, there were some bright spots. We saw Celia Johnson and

Trevor Howard in that quintessential English film, *Brief Encounter* which had just been released and went to all the local dance band venues.

There was very little to do on the Station and, after the excitement of the war I quickly got bored. Occasionally I would be asked to test fly the Oxfords after they had been serviced but otherwise there was very little flying to be done. One job which did require attention though was to clean up the Headquarters building at RAF Castle Combe. The staff had left in rather a hurry and the place was a mess so the Group Captain asked me to take a squad over there and tidy it up. I took a Corporal, a Flight Mechanic and three general duty airmen and flew over to the airfield. As I brought the Airspeed Oxford in to land it felt strangely nostalgic even after just a few weeks, to fly back into the Base where Joy and I had met.

I set the men to work under the watchful gaze of the Corporal and I went outside and breathed in the summer air: already the Base had the feel of an abandoned aerodrome. I looked around and apart from our Oxford, there was only one other aircraft left. There was no roar of engines, no shouted commands from Flight Sergeants, no sound of erks doubling across the concrete: instead there was peace and calm. The grass had begun to grow, the birds were singing and an unlocked door was gently banging in the easy breeze. I wandered over to my faithful Auster and walking around her, thought of our last flight together: it would be nice to do it again. In 1995 when Joy and I revisited Castle Combe as VIP guests of the owners and I found out what had happened to her, I could have cried; a tragic end to a wonderful little aeroplane. Had I known what her fate was to be I would have bought her from the RAF there and then.

I looked over to the control tower and thought about my meeting with Joy just a few months before and of how much had happened and changed in that time; we had met, fallen in love and married; the war had ended, the Base had closed and peace was really here for the first time in six long and dangerous years.

My reverie was broken by the sound of the Corporal's approach. I returned his salute and he told me that the base Headquarters was ready for inspection. We walked over to the utilitarian building and I was pleased with the hard work which the airmen had done to tidy the place up. I thanked them all for their effort and we clambered back into the Oxford and returned to Brize Norton: thus I became the last serving pilot to take off from RAF Castle Combe Advance Training Station. It would be 50 years before I returned.

By the end of 1946 there was no more excitement and I was bored; I took my own advice and left the Service. I had been in the RAF for more than seven years and now I was back in Civvy Street. I had left home in 1939 as a 19 year old lad; now I was almost 27, had grown up, been to war and had a wife to provide for. That was my next challenge and I had no idea how I was going to meet it.

A   B   C   D   E

a) Distinguished Flying Cross: for courage and devotion to duty against the enemy.
b) 1939-45 Star: for service under operational command
c) Atlantic Star and bar: for operational flights over the Atlantic; bar for Aircrew Europe operational command whilst holding the Atlantic Star.
d) Defence Medal: for three years service in UK
e) War Medal (Victory Medal): for Armed Forces Service.

Chapter 13
Starting Over and Making Out

Seven years in the Services is a long time and I had grown used to the idea that everything was provided for me or heavily subsidised. Now I had to make a fresh start and provide for Joy. I decided to go back to my old profession and at the beginning of 1947 I applied to Sandwell Council in Birmingham for the post of Architectural Assistant. They offered me the job and then they offered me £4-10-6 [£4.52½ p] a week to do it. We couldn't live on that; I declined the offer.

At this time Joy and I were living at mother and father's house in Shrewsbury and on the night of 24th January 1947 it started to snow; and it snowed every day and night until 16th March. Along with most other rivers in the Country, the Severn, Britain's longest river and the Thames both froze, industry shut down, roads everywhere were blocked, drifts of ten feet or more were commonplace, communities were cut off and the RAF was called in to air drop supplies to them; I was so envious because as a bomber pilot I would have been doing that job. When the snow stopped on the 15th March, the Ides of March, it was followed by a thaw and a great storm the following day which caused dreadful floods everywhere. But eventually the weather improved and 1947 was one of the loveliest summers on record.

Inevitably after the war, a lot of reconstruction work started as bombsites were cleared and new housing was built for the returning troops. It was dangerous work; as the sites were cleared the discovery of an unexploded bomb was a fairly regular occurrence and more than a few blew up as they were disturbed. Looking for work, I realised that there was a distinct advantage to using my rank in applications. Society was very different then and was conditioned to a hierarchical attitude. I joined Prefabricated Constructions Limited of 11, Upper Grosvenor Street, West 1 as its General Manager and we took a flat in Streatham Common. The company made those prefabricated homes which sprung up all over Britain, supposedly temporary housing with a ten year life span: many are still going strong today and some have even been designated as Listed Buildings under the planning regime. The prefabs had an aluminium frame, outer walls and roof and could be erected in 4 hours. Between June 1945 and December 1946 nearly four million service men and women were demobbed and most of them needed somewhere to live.

It was whilst I was with Prefab Ltd, as we knew it, that Felicity, our first child was born. By now it was summer time and I had had enough of working in London. It was hot, full of traffic fumes, expensive and commuting was a chore; nothing has changed about that in 60 years! I needed to get out and so I resigned. The three of us left Streatham and moved back to my parents' house in Shrewsbury. That's what people did then in the days before easy mortgages.

I had no idea what I was going to do and our meagre savings were beginning to dwindle fast. One night I saw an advertisement in the Shrewsbury Chronicle for a Sales Representative with the agricultural merchants, Bates and Hunt (Agric.) Limited. That would do nicely I thought but I knew nothing about selling and even less about agriculture. No doubt on the strength of my Squadron Leader's rank and my DFC, I had been called for interview so I went to Shrewsbury Library and borrowed two books on agriculture. In the days beforehand I studied these books carefully and was satisfied that I could answer any technical problem which they threw at me at the interview. There were five of us up for the job and we all sat in a downstairs room waiting to be called on the tannoy speaker up to Ken Hunt's office. After the last one came back downstairs we waited expectantly for the result. When it came, it was announced over the tannoy for the whole office complex to hear. "Attention please. Would Mr Don Gatley please come up to the office and would Squadron Leader Cowling wait behind. The rest may go. Thank you for attending Gentlemen".

I knew that I had not got the job but wondered why I had been asked to wait behind. I didn't know it then but that day was to direct my life for the next 40 years or so. After a short time I too was summoned back up the stairs. Ken Hunt told me that he knew that I had no agricultural experience but had been so impressed with my theoretical knowledge, together with my war record, that he wanted to offer me a job as a trainee salesman. With no other job in sight and a family to support I accepted his offer.

For the next 12 months I worked and trained on Ken's farm at Buckatree Hall, where his manager Eric Pell who sadly died only last year in 2004, taught me to drive a tractor, plough a field, milk a cow and a hundred other jobs around a farm. I was also learning about grain, the different types, what each was used for, what was good grain and what wasn't and so on. During this time Joy and I also became close friends with Ken Hunt and his wife, Barbara.

At the end of my 12 months training I went on the road as a travelling salesman and became very good at my job. It occurred to me though that I had no formal qualification in this business and so I enrolled at Cirencester Agricultural College and the National Institute of Agriculture and Botany at Cambridge. At the end of these courses I was a qualified Crop Inspector and Seed Analyst. By now Joy and I, together with baby Felicity had moved out of my parents' house and into our own home off the Roman Road in Shrewsbury.

Ken Hunt was a great socialiser and we regularly joined he and Barbara for an entertaining night in their home at Buckatree Hall. One night as he and I were standing in the cloakroom he handed me a one-pound note and said, "Here you are Ted, take it." I took it and then he said, "Right, give it me back". I returned the note to him not having a clue what he was playing at. "Ok Ted, you have now got a £1 share in the business and will join the board of directors as from tomorrow and be registered as a director of the company". He made me Sales Director.

Even before the war had started, the government knew that one of its biggest problems would be to have enough food to feed everyone and that the U-boat blockade, against which the Battle of the Atlantic was so bravely fought, could quickly starve us into submission. As a result, in October 1939 the Agriculture Minister of the day Sir Reginald Dorman-Smith, broadcast to the Nation about the importance of growing as much of our own food as possible. 'Dig for Victory' became the best known slogan for this message and was first used in this October BBC Home Service broadcast. Allotments, flowerbeds, lawns, even town parks were turned into vegetable plots. As a result by 1945, much more of Britain's countryside was under cultivation than it had been in 1938. Consequently the newly elected Labour government of 1945–1951, not only introduced various social reforms, but also embarked upon a strategy of trying to make Britain self sufficient in those crops which the climate allowed us to grow, and grain was one such crop.

It is an interesting reflection upon the change in our social values in just 65 years, that there was very little theft from these town park allotments, partly due no doubt to the fact that the theft of such war materials potentially carried the death penalty, and there was no vandalism at all. We were literally fighting for our very survival. It is a sad reality of today that any vegetables grown in such a public place in a town or city would so inevitably be mindlessly vandalised or stolen that no one would attempt to grow them.

About this time the agro-chemical industry was really getting going and with government blessing. So by the late 1940's crop spraying was the thing to do to reduce pests and increase yields. Now on the board of directors, I helped Ken to set up Bates and Hunt (Crop Spraying) Limited. One lovely summer day we drove down to Swindon to meet Bill Barratt, a retired engineer and Chairman of the firm Evers and Wall, which made crop sprayers. Over a splendid lunch at a country pub we discussed the details of how we could attach the sprayers to the twelve Land Rovers we had bought from the Shrewsbury car dealers, Vincent Greenhous. How the pub produced food like that I don't know because rationing was still very firmly in place. I suppose that was the difference then between living in the country and living in the towns and cities.

Bill Barratt was an interesting character and in addition to the chairmanship of Evers and Wall Limited, he was also the Chairman of Goya Lipstick Limited, which at that time was a major cosmetics manufacturer. Indeed it had been Barratt who had financed Douglas Collins, his next-door neighbour when he lived in Brighton. Collins produced scent from rose petals collected from his own bushes by adding them to a liquid in separate phials which he stored in the shed at the bottom of his garden. During the war Doug Collins had sold these phials of scent to Selfridges in London's Oxford Street, where the American GIs soon snapped them up as presents for their English girlfriends. From these small beginnings the internationally successful Goya Lipstick Company Limited was forged. After the war, Bill Barratt resigned from the Board of Goya and Doug Collins sold the company to Reckitts for over £1,000,000, which was a huge sum of money in those days.

Collins left Goya and wrote his autobiography called "A Nose for Money". Not long after the book was published his daughter was married and in an indulgent gesture to her favourite colour he had his Bentley sprayed pink just for the occasion. Whilst she was on her honeymoon he had it resprayed black. He later bought Sutton's Seeds of Reading and offered me the Managing Directorship of the company. Although I was sorely tempted by the offer, I was by then running my own very successful business in Shropshire and managing Sutton's would have meant moving away from home and all the disruption to our family life which that would have entailed. I was content where I was.

Bill Barratt was very wealthy but was also an astute businessman. I was to be in touch with him again much sooner than I could ever have imagined as we sat around the lunch table of that comfortable country Inn. I worked hard and in a fairly short space of time the contract spraying business became very successful, with all our Land Rovers working flat out. It was simple really; we had got in ahead of the opposition and because most farmers needed their crops sprayed but could not afford the capital outlay on the equipment nor had time to learn the skills to use it, we scooped up the business. Ken Hunt had many businesses in addition to the agricultural corn merchant and spraying companies, including the Buckatree farm, several chemist shops, an Accountancy firm in Wellington's Market Street and a coffee and tea plantation spraying business in Kenya, which was managed by John Nicklin. Not long after this meeting with Bill Barratt, Ken announced that he was selling up in England and moving out to Kenya. He sold the agricultural corn merchant business to the Radnorshire Company Limited, the then chairman and managing director of which was Colonel Hubert Watkins, MC.

I first met Watkins over lunch. Out of the blue one day Ken rang me at the office, asked me to join him at the Red Lion on the A5 Watling Street in Wellington and introduced me to the new chairman of Bates and Hunt. It was quite a surprise but having been instantly suspicious of Watkins, I did not let my reaction show. He was a large man with an attitude to match and still conducted himself as a full Colonel. We sat at the lunch table and discussed Watkins' various plans for the new company, none of which really seemed to impact badly upon my position. At one point he drew heavily on his fat cigar and as he brushed the ash from his large waistcoat covered corporation said, "Of course you will be alright Ted, you will stay on as Sales Director". I was happy enough with that and went home to Joy with the news of what that day had turned up.

That night as we sat in the lounge at Buckatree Hall having our usual after dinner drink, with Joy and Barbara chatting to a couple of their friends in another room, Ken told me that he needed to get out to Kenya for the sake of his health. "You and Joy have been good friends to us Ted and I've really enjoyed working with you. It was a good day when I appointed you but I've lived life a bit too fast and I need to slow down. Kenya will be good for me. I don't want you to worry though because part of the deal with Watkins is that you stay on as Sales Director." With that he got us two more large whiskies: so much for his health and slowing down!

Up until then Ken had run the business as a family concern in which he knew all his employees by name. Once the Radnorshire Company took over that atmosphere disappeared overnight. Just 14 days later, with Ken still on his way to Kenya, Hubert Watkins summoned me to his office and told me to sit down. There was no courtesy in the man and I just knew that this was going to be bad news. Puffing away on his ubiquitous fat cigar he said, "I'm reorganising things here Cowling. I'm going to put you on the road as our fertiliser salesman". For a moment I couldn't take in the words he was saying. I just stared at him and then the significance of it dawned on me. If he thought he was going to treat me like that he would think again. I stood up and turned towards the door, "You bloody well won't," I said, "you can sell your own shit". I walked out of his office and as I turned to make sure that I had left his door as wide open as I could, my last sight of the man was of him sitting behind his huge desk, his cigar almost falling out of his fat hand, his mouth open and by the colour of his face, his blood pressure rising dangerously fast.

I went back to my own office and quickly threw my personal possessions into my brief case. This was long before the days of mobile phones, laptops, electronic diaries and the like, so it didn't take me many minutes; and I was angry. I told Muriel Taylor what Watkins had said to me and what my reply had been. I thanked her for her work and I left the building. As I got into my car I vowed to myself that Watkins would need me before ever I needed him.

Chapter 14

In Business

That night I telephoned Bill Barratt at his home in Ross-on-Wye and asked him if he would be interested in investing in a seed merchant business in Shropshire. He appeared to be very interested and the following day I arranged for him to stay at the Mytton and Mermaid Hotel at Atcham, where we were able to discuss my proposition in more detail.

After I had left Watkins' offices, I had gone to a quiet pub to think through what I was going to do next. I knew this business very well now, and more importantly, I knew nearly all the farmers in Shropshire. I made up my mind, finished my drink and went home to talk my plans through with Joy. She thought it all sounded a good idea and gave me her support and the encouragement I wanted from her.

Barratt had a threshing contractors business in Newport, Monmouthshire which had ceased trading. He became the chairman of the new company, I was the managing director and we opened as Barratt's [Agric] Limited, from offices in Roushill Bank in Shrewsbury the following week. The morning after my meeting with Bill Barratt, I rang Muriel Taylor and asked her to come and be my secretary. She had always been very good at her job and I needed someone who knew the business and whom I could trust. She readily accepted and joined me immediately: within a fortnight her husband, who was Watkins' Transport Manager at Bates and Hunt also left to join us. I rented Dick Harris's stackyard at Home Farm, Atcham and a few days later Tom Earp, a sales representative and malting barley buyer at Watkins' Radnorshire Company, also left to join me. I knew that Tom was the best at his job and I gave him 10% of my shares and a seat on the board of directors. Soon after that Pat Bell, Radco's main barley buyer also joined us as a director.

They were both big losses to Watkins who was furious. He rang me up one day and accused me of trying to put him out of business by taking all his best people. I told him that he should have thought about that when he decided to turf me off the board of directors at Radco and send me out selling fertiliser. This was business and we were doing extremely well. He slammed the phone down and never spoke to me again. My two co-directors Tom and Pat, together with Muriel, her husband Lou as Transport and Mill Manager and myself, gelled into a very happy and efficient team and the business went from strength to strength.

In late 1949 I bought Brittain's Bakery in Wellington's Haygate Road from Bill Morris of Morris & Company Limited Shrewsbury, for £5,000. For an extra £500 I could have had the four adjacent cottages too but the housing market wasn't what it is today and another £500 was a lot of money. We built a new office block and installed seed cleaning equipment, mixers, a grain drier and other essential machinery. At that time we ran a fleet of four of the new articulated lorries and had five Reps on the road together with our mill staff at Haygate Road including the foreman Jack Powell, who had also deserted Hubert Watkins to join us.

The four years after the war had been fairly austere although we had fared better than many. The welfare state had arrived, the railways, the coalmines and the Bank of England were all nationalised and in 1948 the Olympic games had been held in London, giving a much-needed lift. The personality of the Games had been 30-year-old Dutch athlete and mother of two, Fanny Blankers-Koen who had won four gold medals. As the decade turned though things began to improve; rationing was coming to an end and the influence from America was to be seen in the household goods which started to appear in the shops, for those who could afford them.

Susan Joy, our second daughter was born in 1950.

By 1951 we were buying most of the grain grown in

Shropshire and a lot from west Staffordshire too. The business was so successful that we had already outgrown the Haygate Mill site, so I started to look for alternative premises. One of my customers was the farmer RO Griffiths of Duncote Farm at Walcot and on a dreary Monday morning at Wellington cattle market, where Morrison's supermarket now stands, Tom Earp, RO and I were all leaning over the rails of a pen looking at the heifers waiting to be auctioned. As usual RO was complaining about the poor price the animals were fetching when Tom had a brilliant idea. He asked RO if he would sell us some land next to the road at Walcot. He did and on one and a half acres of land at Duncote, between the road and the railway line we built a brand new mill and office block. We sold the Haygate Mill to Freddie Fry the founder of Furrows, for £25,000 and moved all the equipment to Duncote and in addition bought new grinders and mixers. We built new silos and an on-floor drying unit to hold 8,000 tons of grain.

We were the only private cattle feed cubing and pelleting plant in Shropshire and our major customer at this time was the Harper Adams Agricultural College at Edgmond. We manufactured all the concentrated crumb and pellet feed for their very large poultry unit.

As we continued to grow, purchasing ever-increasing quantities of malting barley, we were able to sell directly to the brewing giants Bass and Albrew Maltsters whose brewery was a Ditherington in Shrewsbury. By the mid 1950s we employed 10 reps, many more office and Mill workers and had increased the transport fleet to 8 articulated vehicles and 2 tankers.

In 1955 our son Stephen was born.

The 1950s was a decade of great change and discovery in the world and life in Britain reflected that change. Although it continued at a hectic pace throughout the 1960s, it was a less certain change. During the 50s it was more dramatic and focused because of the very low base from which we started. After the war Britain was so bankrupt that it was included as a beneficiary in the American Marshall Plan which set out to rebuild the conquered Nations of World War II, so that the mistake of the retribution wreaked upon the German population in particular after the First World War was not repeated. Nevertheless during the second half of the 1940s it was sometimes difficult to tell that we were not still at war, except that the bombing had stopped. Rationing continued for many years and life was pretty austere. In fact Britain went back to war in 1948 when the communists invaded Malaya.

But by 1950 there was a real feeling of optimism that perhaps the worst was behind us, even if we still had rationing and the West Germans did not! Sainsbury's opened Britain's first supermarket and King George VI opened the Festival of Britain; a new Queen was crowned and Mount Everest was conquered; the music charts appeared and rock'n'roll was born; National Service ended and the Archers began; the Lord of the Rings was published and *The Mousetrap* began its phenomenal run in the West End; Britain launched the world's first nuclear submarine, the *Nautilus* and the Soviet Union launched the world's first space satellite, *Sputnik 1*; Cold War relations iced over and the Suez crisis boiled over; a plane crash at Munich airport killed eight of the Manchester United 'Busby's Babes' football team including Duncan Edwards and Tommy Taylor, and scientists James Watson and Francis Crick discovered the double helix structure of DNA; the European Common Market was formed, without Britain, a hovercraft crossed the English Channel and Premium Bonds, postcodes, parking meters and motorways arrived.

The 1950s were not perfect years but they belonged to a much more innocent age and I believe we are poorer as a society for the passing of their spirit and culture. No wonder that Prime Minister Harold Macmillan's 1959 election slogan was "You've never had it so good": and history has shown that he was absolutely right.

Chapter 15

Ring in the Changes

The deal which I had struck with Bill Barratt was that although he was the Chairman of the company, he would not interfere and would leave the running of the company to me together with the day-to-day management of it. We had divided the shares between the two of us on a 50/50 split and we had agreed that if either of us wanted to sell the company, then we would do so. Although today this might seem a strange arrangement in the much more highly regulated world of commerce, back in 1949 when we put the deal together that night at the Mytton and Mermaid Hotel, it was a perfectly reasonable and workable arrangement which suited us both very well.

I had given 20% of my shares to Tom Earp and Pat Bell, making Bill the major shareholder with 50% but not a controlling interest, me with 30% and Tom and Pat with 10% each. We met up with Bill four times a year and over a pleasant lunch would keep him in the picture of how the business was performing and where we were going with it. On one of these occasions in 1961 Bill told us that his wife Anne, had become very ill. She had cancer. Very soon afterwards Anne died and Bill was devastated. At our next meeting Bill announced that he was selling up all his business interests and that he wanted to activate our agreement and sell the company. We were not surprised and indeed had already paved the way for such a move. We started formal negotiations with Rank Hovis McDougall, the conglomerate flour company. Barratt's [Agric] Limited became a wholly owned subsidiary of RHM and I became its Chairman and Managing Director. Tom and Pat stayed with me as directors.

In 1962, with three children aged 15, 12 and 7, Joy and I decided it was time to move out of Shrewsbury and so we bought Allscott House. This was ideal. It had several acres of ground for the children to play in and for the girls to keep their horses on and it was only a mile away from the Duncote Mill. We had many happy years at Allscott House and became involved in the local community. We went to St. Peter's Church at Wrockwardine and every year Joy helped with various parish events including the annual Fete and Garden Party at Wrockwardine Hall.

In 1959 the Morris Mini-Cooper was launched and after the film *The Italian Job* it was the car to be seen in. I bought one for Joy, and Flip and Sue often went out to Shrewsbury in it. One dark Saturday night in 1967 they borrowed the car to go to a party. As usual they were in good spirits and called cheerio as they went through the door. I told them to take care and Joy told them not to be too late. Not long afterwards the telephone rang and I spoke to a man who was ringing from his house. I didn't say anything to Joy except that I was going out. I jumped into my Jag with my heart pounding like never before. When I got to the scene of the accident I could see the mini stuck underneath the trailer of an articulated lorry; there was no roof on the car. The lorry had been stationary across the main road without any lights on and the girls had gone underneath it from the side. I felt sick; I had never experienced these emotions even during the war when I had lost some very close friends.

I got out of the Jag and started to walk towards the wreckage of Joy's car, the smell of petrol and steam filling my nostrils. "Hello daddy. We had rather hoped you wouldn't find out about this tonight." It was Sue. She and Flip were sitting at the side of the road wrapped in blankets, shaken but otherwise unhurt. I couldn't believe that they had walked away from that mess. I wept with relief but the girls were more upset at missing the party and insisted that I took them on to it.

The mini was such a small car and the seats so low to the ground that their heads had been below the side of the trailer. The mini had saved their lives; in a higher car they would both have been killed. Today, artic trailers have guardrails to prevent such an accident.

I stayed with RHM for another ten years but by 1971 the parent company was changing and I could see the writing on the wall, so I left and once more set up my own seed merchant's company, which I ran for several more years. At about the same time I decided to start using some of the land at Allscott House more productively since Stephen was now 16 and the girls were grown up. I got into rearing pigs and at the height of the operation was raising 3,000 at a time.

Muriel Taylor had left RHM with me and was still my secretary in the new business, but we were not grinding grain and manufacturing animals feeds any more; the business now was as wholesalers. Consequently we needed something else to do during the growing season. The pigs filled in some of that time but once set up my pig man saw to that side of things. I decided to start a printing business as a hobby. I knew nothing at all about printing so I did what I had done 25 years earlier back in 1947 when I applied to Ken Hunt for a job: I went to the library, borrowed a book and read all about it. I took out two books and Joy, Muriel and I read them each in turn. Whilst doing this over the period of about a fortnight, we said nothing to each other about printing. When we had all read the books we sat down, talked it through and decided to give it a go. Wrekin Ultraprint was born.

In 1985 I looked around at the corn business I was still in. It had changed out of all recognition in the years since 1947. When I started, I knew all the farmers and they in turn knew me and they owned or rented the land they farmed. By 1985 increasingly the actual land work was being done by contractors, the price was agreed in Brussels and many of the old characters I had known had retired or died or both. I had been a corn merchant for nearly 40 years and it was time I retired too. I sold the business, sold the pigs and decided to have a more sedentary life with just the printing. Wrong.

I was imposed upon and remained as Chairman of the Shropshire branch of the Corn and Agricultural Association for some number of years.

In October 1989 Joy and I received an invitation to attend a reunion dinner at the Park Hall Hotel in Wolverhampton. 210 (Flying Boat) Squadron had formed a retirement association and its secretary, Bill Balderstone, had done a fine job tracking down as many survivors as possible, including me.

We turned up at the Hotel and I dropped Joy off at the front door whilst I went to park the car. It took about ten minutes but by the time I got back to the hotel building there was no sign of Joy. Off I went to look for her in the crowd of people who were filling the big room; I eventually found her with a drink in her hand chatting away to chap with a handlebar moustache. It reminded me of VE night and Joy sitting in my car with Flight Lieutenant Robinson drinking my whisky and I caught myself smiling at the thought. At least this time it wasn't my booze that they were drinking. As Joy handed me the drink she was holding for me, together with my name badge, "Squadron Leader EA Cowling, DFC", she said, "You see that man over there," and indicated to a small, silver-haired chap speaking to half a dozen people around him who were listening very intently. "Well", continued Joy, "he was just saying that he was part of the crew who flew Harry Hopkins to Russia".

I didn't recognise him so I wandered over to the group but he was holding his drink in his left hand and his arm covered up his name badge. When he had finished speaking I said to him, "Joy tells me that you flew with McKinley to Archangel. What's your name then?" He turned to me, looked at me hard and then his face lit up in a wide smile; "Derrick Buley. How the hell are you Ted?" I put my arms around him and we embraced one another with rather watery eyes. My pal Derrick, who we had shoved into the wing of the Sunderland that night and to whom I had passed great quantities of chewed chewing gum to patch up the shrapnel holes in the fuel tanks, had also survived the war. I was delighted and we had more than one drink on the strength of our survival. It had been 48 years since we had last seen each other.

There was a surprisingly good turnout that weekend and we had a wonderful time including a visit to the very good RAF Cosford Aviation Museum, which houses one of only two surviving TSR2s, Britain's secret swing-wing fighter 'plane of the 1960s. The swing-wing technology had been designed by none other than Sir Barnes Wallis and was so far ahead of its time that the Wilson Government of 1964-1970 came under enormous pressure from the Americans to abandon the project for fear that it would put the US fighter programme out of business: the TSR2 was cancelled. At that time I didn't know many of the other members of the Association because most had joined 210 after I had left the Squadron to train as a pilot in 1941 but I did meet a few others whom I had served with including Wing Commander Van de Kiste, Wing Commander Derek Martin, Air Commodore Pearce, still smoking his Sherlock Holmes pipe and blowing out a fountain of lighted tobacco, Bill Miller, our Rigger who had shown me around the Sunderland that first morning at Pembroke Dock back in 1940 and of course Derrick Buley. The Association has met every year since then at various venues around England although as each year passes sadly but inevitably, those attending become fewer.

Once more my plans for sedentary retirement were put back when in 2000 I was elected as Chairman of 210 (FB) Squadron Association.

During my time with the Association I came to realise that so many of those lads who, like me, had joined up at the beginning of the war in 1939 or early 1940 had either been killed or spent many years as a prisoner of war. There were not many of us who had fought all the way through from the beginning and survived outside a prison camp. I had thankfully not become a member of either the Caterpillar Club or the Goldfish Club. I knew that I had been very good at what I had done, which was reflected in my rapid promotion through the ranks from AC2 to Squadron Leader but as the years passed and the wisdom of age triumphed over the exuberance of youth, I knew too that I had also been incredibly lucky.

The Caterpillar Club is formed from that group of men whose lives have been saved by their parachutes in an enforced bale-out. The 'free' parachute, i.e. where the ripchord is pulled by the airman during descent rather than being attached to the aircraft as it is for paratroopers, was invented in 1919 by the American born Leslie Irvin, who at only 19 years of age tested his own invention in front of the US Military. In 1921 Lieutenant Harold R Harris became the first person to be forced to bale out of a doomed aircraft and have his life saved by an Irvin parachute. Since then over 45,000 men have come to owe their lives to Leslie Irvin's invention.

I had almost joined the Goldfish Club that day my Lockheed Hudson had been shot up over the North Sea by the Messerschmitt 110. That is the club of those chaps who had ditched or baled out into the sea and been rescued from the waves, whether by the RAF Air/Sea Rescue Service, the enemy or anyone else. Inevitably many members of the Goldfish Club are also members of the Caterpillar Club. [To source stories of the exploits of members of both these clubs, please see Bibliography].

In the late autumn of 1994 Joy and I were invited to our nephew's wedding near Bath. Returning home the next day we decided in a moment of nostalgic indulgence to call in at Castle Combe airfield which was not very far out of our way. We pulled up at the gates and although they were locked we were pleased to see that the control tower, which had been the scene of our first meeting, had not been demolished as had most of the other buildings. It was Sunday and everywhere was quiet; it felt as it had done 49 years earlier when I had listened to the birds singing whilst the airmen tidied up the Headquarters building. As we stood holding hands in front of the gates, a large car drew up beside my XJS and a well-dressed man got out. We were very obviously not vandals and so he enquired politely, "Can I help you"? I briefly told him why we were standing there and he offered to open the gates and let us in.

He turned out to be Mr Strawford, the Managing Director

of the Castle Combe racetrack company. He took us into his office, made us a cup of coffee and listened with growing fascination as we told him how we had met. He said, "Well the Control Tower is just as it was. We have done nothing to it. Would you like to see it again?" Like two kids we instantly said yes and he took us over to the tower. He opened the door and left us alone to go upstairs. There in the corner of the room was the little wooden hatch which I had opened to get my first glimpse of the lovely girl I would spend the rest of my life with. We were both overcome to be standing in the room where we had first met; to be so consciously revisiting our past from 50 years earlier. As we stood there quietly, each with our own thoughts, those years simply melted away and we were the young RAF pilot and WAAF once more, experiencing the delicious sensations we had that night. Joy told me to open the hatch again and she went round to the other side and kissed me through it. It's a good job she didn't do that in 1945; we would both have been court martialled.

Before we left I told Mr Strawford that I had been the last RAF pilot to fly out of Castle Combe and he asked me to sign the visitors' book, which I did with my name, rank and decoration but no contact address or telephone number. We thanked him for his kindness and hospitality and left with a feeling of childish warmth gleaned from a glimpse into our special past. Apart from the memory of our visit, I thought no more about it.

A few weeks later on Christmas Eve, Joy and I were sitting at home enjoying a drink and ruminating about the family arrangements for the following day when the telephone rang. It was John Gunner, a Flight Engineer from 210 Association. "Merry Christmas Ted. Weren't you the last pilot to fly out of Castle Combe?" he asked. "I was. Why?" "Well they're looking all over for you. When you visited Castle Combe in the autumn you didn't leave your address and they have been putting adverts in all the local papers for you to get in touch." "Who has?" I asked. "The Castle Combe race track people", and he gave me a contact telephone number.

As a result Joy and I went back to the base in February 1995. Mr Strawford had booked us into a lovely local hotel where the staff made us very comfortable and welcome: it was the Castle Inn which had been one of our local pub haunts during the war and to where we had gone on VE night to start our celebrations. Just opposite the Castle Inn had been an old cottage in which lived an equally old couple, who amongst other things kept a few chickens. During the war fresh eggs were a luxury and in the RAF they were reserved for aircrew only. However a shilling [5p] would buy a plate of poached eggs on toast from the old girl at the cottage and jolly good they were too.

The next day we met the Managing Director in his office and after a cup of coffee and a chat he took us down to the old canteen where we were met by an array of reporters and cameramen. After the interviews and photographs we went out onto the runway and with my arms in the air, the television cameras rolled as three Hercules transporters went over very low in a 'fly-past' for me. I was thrilled and not a little emotional about it all. Strawford had also laid on a flight for me and once more I took off from Castle Combe, this time in a Cessna. We flew around the airfield and I took the controls for a while: after all those years the thrill was just the same as the first time I had taken the controls on my initial flying course at Dewinton in Canada 52 years earlier. It was my 75th birthday: what a present.

8 May 1995 was the 50th anniversary of the end of World War II in Europe and Castle Combe had arranged its own celebrations of which Joy and I were to be a part. We were invited back again for the VE day party. I opened the event and was then put into a Swiss armoured personnel carrier and driven around the racetrack waving to the thousands of people who had turned out to take part in the celebrations. What a day it was. As I took off in the Oxford for that last time in August 1945, not in my wildest dreams could I ever have imagined that such an event would take place 50 years later.

Chapter 16

Tears and More Tears

Sue died on 7th February 1992 after her long battle against cancer. We were devastated. She had made a very successful career in television production management and worked for Granada and London Weekend Television. She was such a wonderful daughter and we couldn't believe that she had been taken from us. Her loss affected us deeply and would continue to do so down the years. It made us realise that all the success and happiness which we had enjoyed as a family was, in reality, so very fragile.

By now we had sold Allscott House. The children had all long since left home and it was getting too big for Joy and I. We had kept the paddock and applied for planning permission to build a bungalow for our retirement. We entered the adversarial world of the planning inquiry, solicitors, barristers, planning officers, highway engineers, drainage engineers, landscape architects and of course the incumbent Secretary of State for the Environment, as the job was known as then. Although I didn't know it at the time, this was all good grounding for the challenges which lay ahead.

Despite being represented by an eminent QC we lost that first planning appeal, but later tried again and this time we succeeded, obtained consent and built a bungalow, Penmaric, on the paddock. We then sold Penmaric and built Polkerris at the far end of the paddock, selling the building plot in between the two.

Not long afterwards, the then District of the Wrekin Council decided that it needed to create another caravan site for gypsy travellers and thought that the ideal place for it would be close to Allscott. Fairly naturally there was a lot of local opposition to the proposal, including from the travelling community itself, but we had to go through the planning appeal process. I was elected as the Chairman of the Allscott Action Group and led the campaign to oppose the development. We went to the public inquiry and won. The plans were dropped. Well that's that, we thought.

Not quite; no sooner was the travellers' site seen off than the Council received a planning application from a consortium wishing to build a 'Skypark'. Essentially, this was a major housing development with its own airfield and each house would have, in addition to a double garage, an aeroplane hanger. The idea being that because the roads of Britain are so clogged [no argument with that] the 21st century executive would fly to London, Manchester, Glasgow, Leeds, Europe etc. As a pilot this was an idea which I found very attractive and of course the terrain around Allscott was ideal as there had been many airfields in Shropshire during the war because much of the east and north of the county is very flat. In fact there had been a Relief Landing Ground airfield on part of the site at Bratton and thus the terrain was ideal for the Skypark. But this was not war and many more people now lived under the flight path of this proposal.

The then Chairman of the Planning Committee and the planning officer responsible went off to Florida to see one of these Skyparks in operation and came back prepared to recommend approval. However the Secretary of State called in the application and a public inquiry was arranged. So once more the community joined battle with the planning authority and a gallery of QCs instructed by various other interested parties. The skies above us, which already droned to the sound of the multi-services helicopter training base at RAF Shawbury 5 miles to the north and the 'low-wing' training school at RAF Cosford 10 miles to the east, would be further added to by 49 executives flying in and out each day. Despite the wealth of talent and experience lined up against us we succeeded in persuading the Secretary of State for the Environment that it was not a good idea, at least not in rural Shropshire.

Around this time I met Ken Ballantyne, who has become

a very good friend to Joy and I. I was standing in the lounge bar of the Pheasant Inn at Admaston one evening talking to the landlady, Margaret Wedge and bemoaning of the problems I was experiencing with the tenants of the people who had bought Penmaric from us. There was another man standing at the other end of the bar whom I vaguely recognised but didn't know his name. As I continued with my tale of woe to Margaret she said, "I don't know why you're telling me Ted, you should speak to a solicitor. Why don't you ask Ken what you should do", and she indicated to the man at the bar. "Are you a solicitor?" I said. "I am Ted," he replied. I asked him how he knew my name and he said that everyone knew me; I hadn't expected that answer. I asked him who he worked for and he said, "Wrekin Council". I remembered then where I had seen him before; he had been one of the Council's solicitors at the Skypark Planning Inquiry. I retorted rather too quickly, "I'm not bloody talking to you. You lot are always against me!"

Well Margaret was having none of that. She tore me off a strip and told me not to be so rude to her friend, so I apologised and told Ken all about my problems with the neighbours. He took the papers, helped me out and we successfully sued the owners. Job done. That was the start of our friendship which has not only taken us back to court on occasions but also to various parts of the Country.

On the 12 July 1995 Joy and I celebrated our Golden wedding anniversary and with friends and family we went to the Hadley Park Hotel in Telford. Neither Joy nor I could really say where all those years since that lovely summer day back in 1945 had gone. How different the world was now, how much we had done and how far we had come. As I sat at the table listening to my brother-in-law talking about us to the 50 or so guests we had invited, I let my thoughts drift back over those years. I was 75, I had enjoyed a very happy childhood, apart from some fairly scary missions I had had a good war, married a wonderful girl and had had three lovely children. I had created several successful businesses and was still going strong: I was very happy.

Four years and seven months later to the day, on 12 February 2000 Felicity died from cancer. We just could not comprehend how we could lose both our girls to this dreadful disease. The family which we had created and nurtured through our married life was slowly being taken away from us; what had we done to deserve this. We had only ever tried to help other people and to do our best for our family and our community; why were we being punished so cruelly. I knew that Felicity's loss had finally broken Joy's spirit, but despite our grief we were now to be parents again: Flip's daughter Anna, who was only 16 when her mother died, came to live with us. She finished school, went to university and graduated with a Batchelor of Arts degree. At the time of writing Anna has taken the fashionable 'gap year', enjoying herself with some friends working her way around Australia.

Stephen has remained a loyal and patient son. In spite of the inevitable vicissitudes of his own life he is always there for us when we need him. He has given us two lovely grandchildren in Joseph and Sarah and their visits became one of the few bright spots in our lives. Joy had been so strong for so long but after Anna left home I knew that the pain of the last few years had drained her of any enthusiasm for life. The perfidious gods of love, who had brought us together and given us so much in our lives, had extracted a terrible price for our earlier happiness.

Chapter 17
Celebrities

In 2003 Ken put in train something entirely different for us. The supermarket chain ADSA, together with the cosmetics company Fabergé, on behalf of the NSPCC, ran a competition to find Britain's most romantic couple. Ken nominated Joy and I and told the story of how we had met on that dark, wet February night in 1945 when Joy had talked me down and undoubtedly saved my own life and that of the MO. We won the regional final and joined the other four winning couples from across Britain for the grand final held at the Millennium Hotel in London's Grosvenor Square on St Valentine's Day 2003.

Ken came with us and made a wonderful PA, ensuring that we were always where we were supposed to be when we were supposed to be. We arrived shortly before lunch and decided that, in view of the heightened state of security at that time in London following the atrocities in the United States on 11 September 2001, we were either in the safest hotel in the Capital or the most vulnerable one since the American Embassy was situated only a few yards away and was very heavily guarded.

After a rest we went down to lunch with all the other finalists. We were five very different couples from Scotland, the northwest and northeast of England, the south and the Midlands. Joy and I were the eldest and the couple from the south, in their early twenties, were the youngest. This was when we met Carole and Clive Carrick from the northeast. They are both from Newcastle but live just inside Scotland in their renovated cottage, idyllically set amongst the rolling Berwickshire hills overlooking the fertile lands of the Borders.

They met over 20 years ago when Clive was on leave from the Royal Navy and Carole was nursing. 18 months later and home again on leave, Clive left his parents' home on his motorbike to pick Carole up from the hospital at the end of her shift. It was 9 o'clock at night two days before Christmas. It was dark, cold and wet but Clive was very happy because he and Carole were planning their wedding. Suddenly from a darkened street a car careered out of control and crashed into Clive's motorbike throwing him off it and along the road. The driver was drunk and on his way home from a Christmas party. In the accident Clive broke his back and was told that he would never walk again. His career in the Royal Navy was over and he thought his life with Carole was too, but she was determined to stick beside him and so he resolved to walk down the isle with her on their wedding day: and he did. Two more loving and genuine people you could not wish to meet; an example to us all.

The evening arrived and all the five couples sat around the same table, which made for a very pleasant and convivial dinner which was followed by our various stories being told to the great and the good, all of whom had assembled for the greater benefit of the NSPCC. We were rooting for Carole and Clive and they for us, but in the event the judges voted Joy and I as Britain's most Romantic Couple, something which 58 years earlier on that day in Christ Church in Reading when I was cussing Len for not turning up, I could not have foreseen in my wildest dreams. After the presentations Carole leaned across and congratulated us, adding that they were so relieved not to have won because the prize was a two week holiday and they wouldn't have found anyone to care for all their animals at home which included dogs, cats, goats and chickens.

Joy and Ted with their award

Joy had done so well that night because the media had been telephoning and interviewing us for a week already and now there was more to come. She turned in and left Ken and I to join the party which rolled on into the early hours, in the company of the rich and the famous.

Early next morning the telephone rang in the bedroom and we were live on Radio Shropshire; we were celebrated in the national newspapers and appeared on regional television. After breakfast we took our leave and headed for Euston Station. We left the hotel at 11.30am with the intention of catching the 12.45 through train to Wolverhampton, which gave us a nice connection to Wellington. The taxi got straight through to Euston with hardly a stop. 10 minutes flat instead of the 25 minutes it had taken us the day before. When we got to Euston I'm afraid I just wandered off and up the steps to the main concourse. This meant that Ken was left to carry his own case, my case, Joy's case, my suit bag and Joy's flowers whilst also helping Joy up the steps. Joy was so cross that when they caught up with me at the top of the steps she told me to help Ken and carry something; so without really thinking, I took the flowers from him and wandered off again. Ken didn't say what he thought of that but Joy certainly expressed her opinion!

By now it was 11.50am and there was a train to Wolverhampton standing at platform 3. So we purposefully made our way ½ mile along the platform until in the very front coach we eventually found 3 seats which were neither occupied nor reserved. With Joy and I duly settled and the cases, bags and flowers safely stowed away Ken set about finding out why the train was late and when it would leave. Via the intercom, Donna the Train Manager tried to sooth the passengers. "We apologise to customers for the delayed departure of the 11.15 service from London Euston to Wolverhampton. We hope that this train will be leaving as soon as possible." Click. I had thought that this was the delayed 11.45 but it was actually the even more delayed 11.15. My heart sank. Donna again, but this time somewhat less soothing. "We apologise to customers for the continued delay of the 11.15 service from London Euston to Wolverhampton. This is due to an overhead line fault at Watford Junction. We hope that this train will leave as soon as possible." Click. Ken suggested that we stayed with our bags and he would go and find Donna the Train Manager.

He said he knew where Donna would be and so got off the train and wandered ½ mile back down the platform to the First Class section. Sure enough he found Donna framed in the open doorway, walkie-talkie in hand. She helpfully explained that she knew no more about what was going on than we did because she was getting her information from the platform tannoy system which at that moment burst into life. The overhead lines at Watford Junction were down and the tracks between Euston and Watford were now full of earlier trains and we were not going to leave Euston at all because we had nowhere to go. Ken asked, "Do you have any helpful suggestions Donna which I can repeat to my elderly travelling companions? No? Great!"

Ideally we should have got a taxi across to Paddington from where we could have got a decent train to Bristol or thereabouts with a connection up through Ludlow to Shrewsbury and then to Wellington. A really beautiful journey. The voice behind the tannoy box on platform 3 however had a different solution and was telling us that our tickets would be valid if we transferred to St. Marylebone Station. Transfer to St. Marylebone Station: it all sounded so simple. So Ken came all the way back down ½ mile of platform to the front of the train to tell us the news.

"What's happening?" I asked him. "It's like this Ted ....", he replied and with bags, cases and flowers retrieved we once more trudged back up the ½ mile of platform to the other end of the train where Donna remained surgically attached to the frame of the open door and her walkie-talkie handset. "Thank you Donna, for your most invaluable assistance". The sardonic remark lost nothing in the translation and we were treated to a withering look.

Once more we entered the heaving mass that was the Euston concourse where the mood was one of simple, suffocating resignation. Back down the steps to the taxi rank and just far enough ahead of the game to get a taxi from a rapidly dwindling line. "St. Marylebone Station, please". "What's the problem up there mate?" I explained. "Ah, I wondered why no one had been down for a cab for an hour". Oh well, at least one of us was satisfied at the news.

At a freezing cold St. Marylebone Station and after a miserable taxi ride for which I would have had to pay at least £10 in any fun fare to be made to feel quite so sick, I got the coffee, Joy sat with the bags and Ken went to the information desk.

"Wolverhampton? No mate. Birmingham Moor Street and Birmingham Snow Hill"...... "No mate, it doesn't go to New Street. You'll have to change at Moor Street or Snow Hill"..... "1.45 mate". With over an hour to wait we needed to find Joy an inside seat; she was shivering with the cold. The "Del Gardo" coffee house was of course at the furthest point on the station from the trains. I thought, "blocked lines, late trains, station changes; it wasn't this bad in the war. I haven't been on the railways for sixty years and yet the system has got worse since then. At least this time I won't be on a charge if I'm late back."

In due course we found the last three seats on the crowded local train to Birmingham, which was just as well since we could not possibly have stood for all of that journey. How times have changed: young men apparently thought nothing of remaining seated whilst women had to stand. At that age I had stood for many parts of my train journeys up and down the Country in order to allow a lady to sit down.

2 hours 17 minutes and 11 stops later we got to Birmingham Snow Hill. It's about 10 minutes walk to New Street but Joy and I were too tired to walk it. There are no taxis here so we took the Metro which is close by. 45 minutes and 22 stops later we got to the Wolverhampton terminus strategically located outside the Law Courts. Another taxi ride to Wolverhampton Station.

As we struggled out of this skip on wheels Joy whispered to me that she needed the Ladies. "That's okay," I said, "they're just here by the entrance". 'Out of Order'. I couldn't believe it, not after the journey we had just had. "Platform 2, my mate". At Wolverhampton, Platform 2 is on the other side of the station over the main tracks and involves 4 long flights of steps and then back again. Joy looked even paler and in some desperation. Never mind, we can use the lift, I thought. This is actually the goods lift and, 'Passengers are forbidden to use this lift unless accompanied by a member of the station staff'. "I'll be with you in a minute my mate. I'll just see this train off to Liverpool". I think he must have gone with it to Lime Street. There was no one else about; we were locked into him. We eventually found him again, "Excuse me, but I seem to distantly recall that you were going to try to assist us", said Ken. He got that same withering look we had had from Donna at Euston: I think they must teach it on the customer care course.

We carefully stepped into the old, creaking, wooden goods lift accompanied by the porter. "Where to, my mate?" We were standing in the station goods lift at platform level: where else did he think it could go but up? We were tired, hungry and just wanted to be at home. We did not need a comedian just then but if it served to activate him we would go along with it. "The Ladies powder room and then menswear please", I said without humour. "You can't go in there my mate, ha ha ha". "If you don't get this lift moving quickly we won't need to," Ken rejoined. The porter shut the doors and hummed quietly to himself. "I trust that you will wait to take us back," I said. "Only if you have a return ticket, my mate, ha ha," he replied. Having attended to the necessities, we once again entrusted ourselves to the goods lift and the razor sharp wit of its operator in order to regain platform 1 and our connection to Wellington.

It was now 5.30pm; six hours since we had left the Millennium Hotel. We should have been home 3 hours ago. Our connection which was due now was delayed for 45 minutes. At this point our hitherto resilience and tenacity deserted us and we rang for the cavalry to come and pick us up. We were home by 6.30 just in time to see ourselves on the Regional News at the previous night's award ceremony. It all seemed from another world after our journey from hell.

As I sat by the warmth of my fire enjoying a glass of whisky I reflected upon just how fragile and poor the railways had become in the modernisation process. The total dependency upon electricity to run most of the engines, all the points and all the signals had left the system vulnerable to the slightest trial, tribulation or vicissitude be it from leaves, the wrong kind of snow or just mindless vandalism. If the power went off the whole system ground to a halt. In the days of steam engines and manual points and signals there was no such problem. If the signalman was sick, someone else pulled the lever and the train went on its way. This is not just a romantic notion of a bygone era. On 3 July 1938, the LNER steam engine *Mallard* travelled at 126 mph

[202k/h]. After nearly 70 years of technological advance Britain's trains generally do not come anywhere near this speed, if they run at all! In 1932 the 301 miles from Carlisle to London took 3 hours 15 minutes. 71 years later I had just travelled less than half that distance in more than twice the time. All over Europe the trains run on time and in Japan you can set your watch by them. Why is it that the nation who gave railways to the world is so bad at running them and has the worse network in Western Europe?

By now I had been elected to the Parish Council and had become the Chairman of the Finance and General Purposes Committee. One evening in 2004 I was sitting at home reading through the papers for a forthcoming meeting; the television was on although neither Joy nor I were really watching it with any interest. I had finished with the agenda papers and had changed over the television channel to find some news, when my attention was caught by the start of a programme about a diving club and a wreck in the English Channel. In 1955 the Guinea was officially withdrawn from currency circulation as a coin of the Realm and some sort of commemorative celebration bash was to be held in London. The organisers of this party had commissioned 20,000 half bottles of best champagne, specially labelled and foil seal stamped, 'Golden Guinea'. The bottles were loaded onto a French cargo ship called *The Seine* which duly set off across the Channel to London. On 16 July 1955, about half way through its voyage, *The Seine* was thought to have been in collision with a Russian freighter in stormy seas and sank, taking her cargo of 20,000 bottles of Golden Guinea commemorative champagne to the bed of the English Channel with her. Sailors are very superstitious and whilst I do not know whether the name *The Seine* has been given to another ship, if it has, I suspect that finding a crew may be difficult. In 1900 the previous ship to carry that name, a French bounty cutter, was also wrecked off the British coast. Not an auspicious history.

There she lay, upright and undisturbed in about 120

feet of water until the 501 Divers of Folkestone brought a few bottles up in 1988. The interest in *The Seine* was resurrected in 2004 when the Club, complete with Sky News film crew, went down once more and brought up some of the champagne. There was a formal expert tasting at a top London Hotel and the champagne was declared eminently suitable for drinking, "although there was just a hint of a fishy aroma and taste...." Well there would be, wouldn't there? It had just been sitting at the bottom of the English Channel for fifty years! What a great story I thought and wouldn't it be really different if Joy and I could have some of that champagne for our 60th wedding anniversary dinner in July 2005. So I set about trying to trace the diving club. The television station was willing to disclose nothing and the top London Hotel was even less helpful. It took me two days of telephone calls to every diving club in the south of England, but I eventually tracked down the right one: it was the very last club on my list.

I spoke to the club Dive Master and explained what I wanted it for. He told me that since the Sky News broadcast he had been contacted by people from all over the world asking for some of this champagne but he had refused to enter into any negotiations about it. The find had been reported to the Receiver of Wreck. Nevertheless he was very interested in our story and kindly offered to donate a few bottles to us as a diamond wedding gift if I would go down to Canterbury to collect them. It was too far for me to drive all that way but Ken offered to take me and so in November 2004 we drove down and collected our present. At the time of writing the bottles are sitting in Ken's beer and chocolate fridge keeping nice and cool waiting for July 12th.

Ted and Joy today

My life has been a roller coaster of experiences and emotions. I have known ecstatic happiness and devastating sadness; I have tasted the sweetness of success and smelled the acidity of death; I have lost two daughters to disease and countless friends to machinegun fire; I have thrilled to the pure unadulterated pleasure of flying my little Auster above the Wiltshire countryside and I have sweated with unadulterated fear as fighters and flak have riddled my Wellington bomber 10,000 feet above the German Ruhr; I have been decorated and feted, admonished and berated but throughout it all I have always tried to live by the maxims my parents taught me. There have been so many times that my life could have ended when, in the words of John Gillespie Magee, I put out my hand and touched the face of God: but thankfully each time, He sent me back.

Per Ardua Ad Astra indeed.

- ooOoo -

Squadron Leader Ted Cowling, DFC

The Author

Ted enlisted in the RAF on 4 September 1939, with a burning desire to fly. He was posted as aircrew to Bomber Command and then Coastal Command. Here in 1941, he was part of Churchill's hand picked crew who flew Franklin D Roosevelt's personal envoy to Russia to meet Stalin just days after Hitler had opened the Eastern Front. On his return he was sent to Canada to train as a pilot. Posted back to Bomber Command, he flew Wellingtons over occupied Europe and Germany's industrial heartland. In 1944 and back with Coastal Command, he won the DFC for saving the lives of his crew after being shot up by a Messerschmitt 110 over the North Sea. Later that year he was posted to Training Command where he became a 'Top Gun' Instructor and met his future wife on the night he should have died. He left the RAF at the end of 1946 with the rank of Squadron Leader. He studied Agriculture at The National Institute of Agricultural Botany, Cambridge and The Agricultural

College, Cirencester. In 1948 he became a director of Bates & Hunt (Agriculture) Ltd and in late 1949 he formed his own company which became one of the largest private seed and malting barley businesses in Shropshire. In 1970 he sold out to RHM. Although successful in other business ventures, personal tragedy was to haunt Ted and his wife, Joy. Now retired, he continues to devote his time to voluntary work and in 2003 he and Joy attained celebrity status when they were judged to be Britain's most romantic couple. In 2005 they celebrated their diamond wedding anniversary.

Bibliography

The World at War; The Reader's Digest, published by Reader's Digest Association Limited, 1989
Life on the Home Front; The Reader's Digest, published by The Reader's Digest Association Limited, 1993
Yesterday's Britain; The Reader's Digest, published by The Reader's Digest Association Limited, 1998
The Reader's Digest Atlas of the World; The Reader's Digest, published by The Reader's Digest Association, 1987
Shropshire Airfields; Alec Brew and Barry Abraham, published by Tempus Publishing Limited, 2000
The Illustrated History of the 20th Century; published by Grenville Books Ltd., 1994
Shrewsbury, Pictures From The Past; The Shropshire Star, published by Breedon Books Publishing Co. Ltd., 2001
Jump For It!; Gerald Bowman, published by Evans Bros Ltd., 1955 and by Pan Books Ltd., 1957 [The Caterpillar Club]
A Drop in the Ocean; John French and Jim Burt Smith, published by Leo Cooper [The Goldfish Club]
High Flight; John Gillespie Magee
World Aircraft-World War II-Part 1;Angelucci and Matricardi, published by Book Club Associates, 1978
The Royal Air Force; Michael Armitage, published by Brockhamton Press, 1998
Halifax and Wellington; Bowyer and Van Ishoven, published by the Promotional Reprint Co. Ltd., 1994

Printed in Great Britain
by Partnership Publishing Limited
2 Crown Street, Wellington, Telford, Shropshire TF1 1LP
Tel: 01952 415334
Cover Design: James Baylis
2005